CHRIS C. PINNEY, D.V.M.

GUIDE TO
HOME PET
GROOMING

WITH FULL-COLOR PHOTOGRAPHS
DRAWINGS BY SANDRA G. PINSON AND
MICHELE EARLE-BRIDGES

BARRON'S

636.7083
Pin

About the Author

Chris C. Pinney, DVM, is the author of eight books and has served as veterinary host and adviser for television news magazines and syndicated radio talk shows. He practices veterinary medicine in Houston, Texas.

Acknowledgments

The author wishes to thank the following individuals for their contributions: David Chester, DVM, MS, for his professional expertise and input; Claudia Chancellor and Albert Cisneros for their cosmetic grooming guidelines; Fredric L. Frye, DVM, MS, and Kerry V. Kern for reading the manuscript and making many valuable suggestions; Sandra G. Pinson, Jill Mathis, and Dennis Dunleavy for their artistic contributions; and my wife, Tracy, for her patience.

Photo Credits

Norvia Behling: vi, 2, 3 (top), 4, 5, 6, 9, 13, 15, 16, 18, 21, 37 (left), 40 (top and bottom), 42, 43, 44 (bottom left and right), 46 (right), 52, 53; Cheryl Ertelt: 3 (bottom), 49 (top), 50 (top and bottom), 56 (bottom); Tara Darling: 22, 25 (top and bottom), 33 (left), 38 (left), 46 (bottom left), 47 (right), 48 (left); Dennis Dunleavy: 19 (left, right, and bottom), 20 (top and bottom); Daniel Johnson: 8, 24, 34, 35, 38 (right), 44 (top), 45 (left), 47 (left), 57; Isabelle Francais: 106; Pets by Paulette: v, 23, 31, 39 (left and right), 45 (right), 46 (top), 48 (top), 51, 110; Texas A&M University: 33 (right), 37 (right), 49 (bottom), 75, 80, 81, 82, 83, 88, 89, 91, 93 (top and bottom, 94, 95, 96, 100, 101, 103; Toni Tucker: 10, 26, 55, 56 (top).

Cover Photos

Front cover: Norvia Behling; Inside front cover: Norvia Behling; Inside back cover: Pets by Paulette; Back cover: Norvia Behling.

All inquiries should be addressed to:
Barron's Educational Series, Inc.
250 Wireless Boulevard
Hauppauge, New York 11788
www.barronseduc.com

International Standard Book No. 0-7641-2847-7

Library of Congress Catalog Card No. 2004059670

Library of Congress Cataloging-in-Publication Data

Pinney, Chris C.
    Guide to home pet grooming : complete bathing, grooming, and trimming instructions for dogs and cats including advice on first aid, parasite control, and coat and skin care / Chris C. Pinney ; with full-color photographs ; drawings by Michele Earle-Bridges.—2nd ed.
        p. cm.
    Includes bibliographical references and index.
    ISBN 0-7641-2847-7
    1. Dogs—Grooming. 2. Cats—Grooming. 3. Dogs—Diseases. 4. Cats—Diseases. 5. Veterinary dermatology. I. Earle-Bridges, Michele. II. Title.

SF427.5.P56 2005
636.7'0833—dc22   2004059670

Printed in China
9 8 7 6 5 4 3 2 1

Important Note

This book is intended to enable pet dog and cat owners to groom their pets themselves without seeking the services of a professional groomer. There are many reasons to groom one's pet oneself. Regular grooming sessions enhance the all-important human-animal bond and also allow the owner to discover any developing skin or coat problems and bring them to the attention of their veterinarian. By grooming a pet dog or cat at home, the owner will help the pet to better health and condition than if all the grooming was left to a professional.

A regularly groomed cat or dog is much more pleasant to be around. A well-groomed pet will be cleaner than a neglected one, is likely to shed less and will never be matted or give off offensive odors.

Good grooming should begin when a pet is very young and should always be conducted in a humane and caring manner. There are many grooming operations a "hands on" pet owner can do at home. It just takes a little practice and will not only result in a happier, healthier pet, but it will save the pet owner money and save the pet stress. Try it.

Contents

Preface

Congratulations! You've just taken the first step toward a healthier pet. Using the *Guide to Home Pet Grooming,* you'll learn the easy and correct way to care for your dog's or cat's skin and hair coat. You'll also learn about common skin diseases and disorders, and how to recognize and manage them before they get out of control.

When applied to dogs and cats, *grooming* is a much misunderstood term. Grooming involves more than the weekly trip Bo Bo makes to the local doggie beauty salon, or the decision about which color nail polish Fifi should wear with her red satin sweater. Grooming is not only a way to cosmetically "beautify" dogs and cats and maintain breed standards, but also a significant part of your pet's preventive health care. Did you know that the majority of pet health problems seen by veterinarians involve the skin or hair coat? Many of these challenges could have been avoided if the owners had recognized the need for routine grooming—not at the local grooming shop, but in the pet's home environment. Pet owners can use grooming techniques to help maintain and improve their pets' overall health. It is no accident that beautiful hair coats and supple skin seem to come naturally to healthy animals!

The Guide to Home Pet Grooming focuses on those grooming fundamentals that pet owners can use in their own homes, including brushing; bathing; ancillary care of the eyes, ears, nails, and teeth; nutrition; and external parasite control. A section is included that covers dermatopathies, or disorders of the skin and hair, complete with photos and the latest scientific information. Also included are sections on professional grooming techniques for dogs and cats (for those wishing to learn how to keep their pet's coat looking good between trips to the grooming salon) and on first aid for grooming injuries.

Chapter One

A Question of Grooming

Many misconceptions exist about home pet grooming. Let's dispel a few here and now by answering the three most common questions asked by pet owners about this subject.

Question 1: *Animals in the wild never get groomed by people. Why do I need to groom my pet?*

The key word here is wild. Mother Nature does a good job looking after her own in the wild. For example, in the wild, the hair cycle (see page 9) is primarily influenced by the natural change of seasons and therefore occurs with predictability. Natural terrains not only help wear down the nails, but also remove and comb out dead hair from the coat as animals move through thick underbrush and trees. Unlimited exercise and a diet as nature intended certainly contribute to healthy skin and hair coat. Also, the anatomic features of wild animals, such as hair coat length,

As our pets live in our homes, the need to keep them clean, happy, and well groomed is obvious.

tend to be naturally adapted to geographic location and climate.

If you apply the above examples to the average house pet, the reasons for routine grooming should become crystal clear. The artificial lighting found in the home can disrupt or change the natural hair cycle of a pet, and low humidity in the same can dry the skin and cause it to flake excessively. In comparison with natural terrains, carpets and grass are hardly as effective at wearing down toenails or removing dead hair. When it comes to a pet's diet and exercise, table scraps and poorly formulated pet foods often take the place of a well-balanced diet, and the daily exercise program may be a mere 10-minute walk around the block. And finally, dogs and cats are often poorly adapted to the climate and environment in which they are kept. This can lead to increased stress, skin allergies, and other related health problems.

It is not my intent to imply that every wild animal is the picture of perfect health and immaculate grooming, whereas our poor pets suffer from neglect and hair mats. But I think you

This Abyssinian cat is obviously enjoying the attention his young owner is providing through the brush.

get the point. Pet dogs and cats cannot and should not be compared to their wilder counterparts. They must be treated and cared for differently.

Aside from the fact that pets with skin and coats kept in top-notch condition by routine grooming look good and feel good, there are two other great reasons to groom. First, although you may not realize it, your pet savors every second spent with you. That affection may not be as obvious as you would like it to be, but it exists nonetheless. By grooming on a regular basis, you will help fulfill this basic need of your special friend. Second, when working on your pet, you can be on the lookout for any abnormalities that may tip you off to an underlying disease process. Many pet diseases, such as infections, parasites, diabetes, and cancer, can manifest themselves outwardly as skin and hair coat disorders. Therefore, by routinely inspecting your pet you are more likely to discover these problems early, which could, in itself, be lifesaving.

Question 2: *How often should I groom my pet?*

Dogs and cats should be brushed daily to help remove dirt and dead hair. This daily brushing will stimulate the production of natural skin oils and help spread them throughout the hair coat, thereby keeping it shiny and lustrous. Try to devote 5 to 10 minutes daily to this task.

As far as bathing is concerned, pets with normal, healthy skin and coats need only be bathed "as needed." Use your judgment on this. When your indoor pet begins to smell like an outdoor pet or starts to accumulate dirt or dandruff, it is probably bath time. Beware, though: Bathing a healthy dog or cat too frequently, especially with the wrong type of shampoo, could remove natural oils and predispose your pet to dry skin and related skin problems. For animals with normal skin that require more frequent bathing (that is, more than twice per month), you should use only hypoallergenic or soap-free products when shampooing.

If your dog or cat suffers from skin ailments such as allergies or seborrhea, the bathing frequency will probably need to be increased. If your pet is suffering from a skin infection, your veterinarian may prescribe daily baths with a medicated shampoo. Now you may ask, "But didn't you say that bathing my pet so often will dry out its skin?" True, but I was referring to those healthy pets not affected with skin problems. For dogs and cats with skin disease, the benefits of properly treating such a condition far outweigh the risks associated with dry skin. Furthermore, properly formulated medicated shampoos prescribed by your veterinarian should moisturize, not dry out, the skin, even with daily bathing.

In addition to brushing and bathing, your pet's ears, eyes, teeth, and nails will also require regular attention. By giving your dog or cat a mini–physical examination weekly, you will be able to assess your pet's health and grooming status (see page 29). Be sure to use the exami-

Dogs should be bathed only when it becomes necessary and always dried carefully afterward.

Grooming procedures will vary with your pet's type of coat. Know the grooming requirements of the breed you like, and be prepared to provide them on a regular schedule.

nation checklist provided for this purpose and, if necessary, perform any specific grooming task at that time.

Question 3: *I've heard that cats don't need as much grooming as dogs. Is that true?*

Although it is true that most cats are more efficient at grooming themselves than dogs are, this does not exclude them from grooming. There are some differences between the two species that bear noting.

Because they do quite well at keeping themselves groomed, cats almost never need routine cleansing baths. Thank goodness, because as a general rule, most cats do not care

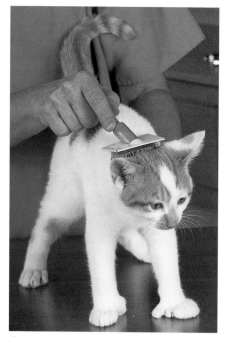

Cats need a gentle touch in any kind of grooming procedure.

to be bathed! Because healthy cats have these meticulous grooming habits, an unkempt, greasy hair coat should alert you that your cat may be ill and needs to be examined by a veterinarian.

Also, feline skin is generally thinner (tomcats excluded!) and, in many cases, much more sensitive than canine skin. As a result, greater gentleness and care must be taken when brushing, combing, or removing mats to prevent injury or irritation to the skin surface. Because cats are so efficient at grooming themselves, you might think they hardly ever need brushing. This isn't true. One excellent reason for brushing your cat regularly is to reduce the incidence of gastrointestinal upset caused by hairballs. It does not matter whether a cat has short or long hair, hairballs can still develop. Furthermore, if fleas, which are known carriers of tapeworms, happen to be ingested along with the strands of hair during self-grooming, your cat could develop a tapeworm infestation. As you can see, brushing your cat on a regular basis is important not only for aesthetic reasons, but for medical reasons as well.

Many shampoos, sprays, and chemicals used commonly and harmlessly on dogs can be toxic and deadly to cats. For example, products containing tar or salicylic acid (aspirin) can be highly toxic to felines if ingested (and keep in mind that cats love to lick themselves, especially after bathing). You must also exercise caution when applying flea

Well-groomed pets are a good reflection on the owners who make sure this part of their care is fully addressed.

and tick insecticides that contain organophosphates, because side effects of these particular chemicals are seen more frequently in cats than in dogs.

The toenails of cats are more fragile than those of their canine counterparts; therefore you must take extra care when trimming them. Be certain the nail clippers you use are sharp to avoid splintering or cracking a nail.

Ear infections are less common in cats than in floppy-eared dogs, primarily because their ears stand erect, allowing air to circulate within the canals and keep them dry. However, this does not mean that you should neglect this aspect of grooming. Always use a drying agent in the ears after bathing and be on the lookout for signs of ear mites or other problems (see "Ear Care," page 31). Of course, there are many other differences, but the benefits afforded by grooming remain the same regardless of the species involved.

Chapter Two

Understanding Your Pet's Skin and Coat

To help you better understand the importance of grooming and the origin of many skin and coat problems, I am going to introduce you to some basic information about the normal anatomy and physiology of the skin and hair. Don't worry: I won't go into great detail, and you may be surprised at what you learn!

The Skin

The skin, the largest organ in the body, is made up of three layers: the epidermis (outer layer), the dermis (middle layer), and the hypodermis (inner layer). Dogs have thinner skin than humans; cats' skin is even thinner. Regardless of the species, the layers of the skin act collectively to perform many important functions. Three of these are protection, temperature regulation, and storage.

Pet owners who understand how the skin and coat protect the animals they cover can better appreciate the importance of keeping the skin and coat healthy.

Protection

The skin protects the body from outside trauma. It also helps maintain the internal environment by preventing the loss of water and nutrients. Glands within the skin (sebaceous glands) secrete oils that lubricate the skin and hair, and also protect against bacterial and fungal infections. The skin of cats and dogs is less acidic than that of humans. As a result, many soaps and shampoos designed for humans can actually irritate and dry out the skin of a pet, even after one use. To be safe, use only those shampoos formulated for dogs and cats, as an inappropriate shampoo can interfere with the skin's protective capabilities.

Temperature Regulation

The skin helps regulate body temperature and protects against rapid temperature changes, both hot and cold, through its hair, blood vessels, and fat. Dogs and cats can't "sweat" like humans can (except through their footpads), so they need to use other methods to keep the body from overheating. Panting is one method you are probably familiar with; another is to

Healthy skin will appear clean and pliant. Owners should report any deviations to the veterinarian as soon as possible.

thereby alerting pet owners to potential health problems early. If skin integrity is lost, or if a skin disease occurs, your pet could be in for a lot of trouble simply because these vital functions will be disrupted. Never ignore a skin problem, no matter how trivial it may seem. You may be observing the mere tip of the iceberg!

The Hair Coat

The coats of dogs and cats come in a variety of lengths, textures, and colors, all of which are largely determined by breed and family genetics. Both species have a primary outer coat, made up of hairs called *guard hairs,* and a secondary undercoat, consisting of much finer, denser *wool hairs.* These wool hairs tend to be much more prominent in cats than in dogs. Long, firm tactile hairs (or whiskers) are found on the heads of both species and on the legs of cats.

The color of the coat is directly proportional to the amount of pigment contained in special cells within the skin and hair follicles called *melanocytes.* For instance, decreased amounts of pigment result in lighter skin and/or hair, whereas an overabundance of pigment causes the skin and/or hair to be darker in color.

Dogs and cats have hair that grows in cycles. This cyclical growth is responsible for the phenomenon we all know as *shedding.* Each hair cycle consists of three phases: *anagen* (the growing period), *catagen* (the transitional period), and *telogen*

trigger an increased flow of blood to the skin to release heat. The hair coat and fatty tissue within and under the skin effectively act as insulation against both heat and cold. One mistake pet owners often make is to shave off the coat of a long-haired dog during the summer months, thinking that this will make the dog cooler and more comfortable. In actuality, the lack of this insulating hair could overburden the skin's ability to regulate temperature and increase susceptibility to heat stroke. When shaving your pet for the summer, don't be too liberal in your clipping. More important, provide plenty of shade and fresh water during the hot months.

Storage

The skin is an ideal reservoir for fat, water, vitamins, proteins, and other nutrients. By serving this function, it also acts as a reliable indicator of a deficiency in any of these items, (the resting period). It is in this latter stage (telogen) that the hairs die and are soon shed. Hair cycles occur in a mosaic pattern: neighboring hair follicles are in different stages of the hair cycle at any one time, so that many cycles are going on at once in your pet's coat. Thank goodness—otherwise your pet would go bald with each shedding cycle!

The main influence on the hair cycle is the change in photoperiod length, or length of daylight. If you consider the way nature intended it, increased shedding should occur during the spring and the fall, thus helping the animal adapt to the temperature extremes to be faced during the upcoming summer or winter months. However, because many pets are kept indoors at least part of the time and are thus exposed to constant degrees of artificial light, nature's rule will not hold true for them. Instead, much to the dismay of their owners, these pets often shed year-round, despite seasonal changes.

Genetics can play a role in the hair cycle as well. For instance, some people claim that certain breeds, such as Poodles and terriers, don't shed at all. In fact, these dogs still shed, but much less so than other breeds. The difference is that these dogs experience a much longer anagen phase than do their peers (anagen-dominant hair cycle), hence shedding is minimal. Conversely, certain breeds can stay in telogen phase for most of the year (telogen-dominant hair cycle) and therefore experience continuous shedding.

Still others experience no such selective dominance of either anagen or telogen, and are considered true seasonal shedders.

In addition to photoperiod and genetics, the hair cycle and shedding can also be influenced by nutrition, disease, environmental temperature, pregnancy, and stress. For example, clipping or shaving can cause the hair cycle to enter into the telogen phase and, in some cases, remain there for a long time (see "Hair Loss Not Related to Disease," page 104). This may explain why hair that is removed for a surgical procedure may take a long time to grow back. Stress can also be a big influence; that is why you will often see dogs and cats shed profusely at the veterinary office (see "telogen defluxion," page 104). This stress-related shedding is actually a defense mechanism in case of attack, designed to leave the attacker with a mouthful (or handful) of hair.

Poodles and certain terrier breeds typically shed less than other dogs and in a different pattern.

Chapter Three

Nutrition for a Healthy Skin and Coat

The old adage "You are what you eat" holds true for dogs and cats. A well-balanced diet is essential for a strong immune system and healthy skin and hair coat (see the table on page 14). Because skin, hair, and nails are in a dynamic state of growth, they constantly require large amounts of nutrients. If a nutritional deficiency is present, the skin and coat are usually the first to suffer. Let's take a look at some essential nutrient groups and find out why they are so important to the *integument* (the skin, hair, and nails).

Proteins and Amino Acids

Proteins and their components, the amino acids, are organic compounds found throughout the body. Their function is to serve as the structural elements for cells, enzymes, hormones, antibodies, and

A well-managed coat begins from the inside. Proper nutrition is a key element in achieving and maintaining a beautiful coat on your pet.

a host of other vital constituents. Although the body is capable of manufacturing most of the specific amino acids and proteins that it needs, it cannot do this without the proper fuel. Where does this fuel come from? It comes from food.

Did you know that up to 30 percent of the daily protein requirement in dogs and cats can be used for the replacement of dead skin and hair? It's easy to see that proteins play a vital role in maintaining the integrity of these regions. Deficiencies can arise from rations that are either low in protein or contain poor sources of protein. Disease conditions such as parasitism or malnutrition can also rob the body of proteins. Signs of protein deficiency can include a dry, rough, thin coat, with or without hair loss (caused by lack of hair replacement); flaky skin; and abnormal shedding cycles.

Adult dogs and cats should have, respectively, at least 20 percent and 30 percent of their daily calories supplied by protein; puppies and kittens, nursing mothers, and pregnant pets need even higher levels. Most commercial dog and cat foods satisfy these requirements; however, not all are the same. Choose a ration that contains protein from more than one food source to ensure that your pet receives a well-balanced blend of amino acids and proteins.

Fatty Acids

If your pet has a dry, lackluster coat, or dry, flaky skin, a fatty acid deficiency may be the culprit. Fatty acids are the compounds that combine to make the oils, fats, and fatty tissue found within the body. Along with providing an important source of energy for their host, they are also vital for healthy skin and hair.

Fatty acids are important components of the oily secretions found normally on the skin and coats of healthy dogs and cats. These oils serve to retain water, thereby keeping the skin moisturized and the hair coat soft. Most fatty acids are manufactured inside the body; certain others are considered "essential"—that is, they cannot be manufactured by the body and must be supplied through the diet. Linoleic acid is an essential fatty acid required by dogs, whereas linoleum acid and arachidonic acid are needed by cats. Most commercial foods have adequate quantities of these; however, deficiencies can occur in dry foods if they are stored over a long period of time (greater than six months).

Certain fatty acids have been shown to be effective anti-inflammatory weapons against allergies in pets. Research has revealed that omega-6 and omega-3 fatty acids can selectively block the pathway leading to inflammation and itching in dogs. When fed at an ideal ratio of 5:1 (omega-6 to omega-3 fatty acids) they can, in some instances, provide partial relief from the itching caused by allergies (see "Allergies," page 83). And the best part: They are safe and relatively inexpensive. Consult your veterinarian for more details.

Vitamins and Minerals

Probably the most misunderstood of all dietary substances, vitamins and minerals are required for normal metabolic and enzyme system function within the body. The vitamins of most importance to the skin and coat of dogs and cats include the B vitamins (thiamine, riboflavin, niacin, and so forth), vitamin A (the retinoids), and vitamin E. The B vitamins, which are considered water-soluble vitamins (vitamins that are not stored by the body) are necessary for the effective metabolism of proteins, fats, and carbohydrates within the body, and the incorporation of these substances into the integument. As a result, deficiencies in one or more of these vitamins can have profound effects. The coat often becomes thin and fragile, and loses its luster. Hair loss can also occur as the skin becomes dry, scaly, and thickened. Once such a deficiency is recognized, supplementation can be used to reverse the symptoms.

Vitamin A, a fat-soluble vitamin (a vitamin that is stored by the body), belongs to a group of compounds known as *retinoids*. These substances are vital to the integument. Among other functions, retinoids regulate metabolism and growth within epithelial tissue. Retinoid deficiencies can create marked changes in the skin. Such deficiencies leave the skin thickened, greasy, scaly, and highly prone to infection. Retinoids have been used for years in human medicine to treat a variety of skin ailments. Conditions such as seborrhea and other diseases of cornification (see "Diseases of Cornification," page 95) have been successfully treated in a limited number of cases using one or more of these compounds, yet their full therapeutic potential still remains unknown. Yet they can't be used indiscriminately. Overusage of vitamin A and other retinoids can be toxic because of excess storage by the body and can lead to bone disease. As a result, supplementation should be performed only under the supervision of a veterinarian.

Vitamin E is another important fat-soluble vitamin that helps maintain the integrity and function of all body cells, including those of the skin. In addition, it helps guard against inflammation and protects fats from becoming rancid. The significance of this latter function is characterized by the fact that, as far as the skin and hair coat are concerned, a deficiency of vitamin

Proper nutrition is essential to all body structures—even footpads and nails.

E looks strikingly similar to a fatty acid deficiency. Even though a naturally occurring deficiency of vitamin E in pets is rare, it can happen if they are fed rations that have been stored over an extended period of time, or if fed diets that contain large amounts of oils. In regard to the therapeutic uses of vitamin E, it has been medically employed to combat inflammation, demodectic mange, and immune-mediated skin diseases in dogs and cats. Its anti-inflammatory effects in dogs suffering from allergies appear to be of little consequence when used as a sole means of treatment; however, combining vitamin E supplementation with other treatment modalities may improve its effectiveness. Because vitamin E, like vitamin A, is stored by the body, toxicity can result if too much is given at one time. Therefore, as with vitamin A supplementation, give vitamin E to pets only upon your veterinarian's approval.

Important Nutrients for the Skin and Coat

Nutrient	Importance	Signs of Deficiency
Dietary protein and amino acids	Precursors for developing skin and hair	Thin, dry, fragile coat; scaly skin
Dietary fats & fatty acids	Natural components of hair, skin, and oily secretions; anti-inflammatory properties	Dull, dry coat; hair loss; scaly, thickened skin
B vitamins	Protein, fat, and carbohydrate metabolism	Similar to protein and fat deficiencies
Vitamin A	Regulates metabolism in epithelial tissue	Thick, scaly skin; skin infections
Vitamin E	Protects cell membranes; protects fats from rancidity	Similar to fatty acid deficiency; inflammation
Zinc	Component of many enzyme systems; affects protein utilization	Dull, dry coats; crusty skin; hair loss; thickened foot pads

Minerals differ from vitamins in that they are inorganic compounds, whereas vitamins are organic, or carbon-containing. The function of minerals is similar to that of their organic counterparts. As with vitamins, minerals are key components of numerous enzyme systems and compounds within the body.

With regard to the skin and coat, one mineral in particular seems to stand out among the rest: zinc. Zinc is important for protein, fat, and carbohydrate utilization, and deficiencies of this trace mineral can cause dull, dry coats; hair loss; and greasy, thickened skin. As with other nutrients, naturally occurring deficiencies in zinc are rare in pets fed high-quality, well-balanced rations. However, deficiencies can occur in those pets fed calcium supplements, because calcium can interfere with

the absorption of zinc from the gastrointestinal tract. In addition, a genetically based zinc-deficiency syndrome has been recognized in breeds such as Alaskan Malamutes and Siberian Huskies. In these instances, inadequate absorption of zinc from the gastrointestinal tract or inadequate zinc metabolism once absorption takes place is to blame. Fortunately for these dogs, zinc supplementation can be used to overcome this problem and help treat the skin disorders that resulted from the original deficiency.

As you can see, vitamins and minerals are required for healthy skin and hair. However, they should never be used indiscriminately to treat skin disorders. Giving large amounts of one particular vitamin or mineral could actually lead to a deficiency of another (for example, the relationship between zinc and calcium), or to a severe toxic reaction. As a result, supplements should be given only if specifically prescribed by a veterinarian.

Water

Although its importance is often overlooked, proper internal hydration is essential for a healthy integument. Pets that live in a chronic state of dehydration will suffer from poor skin elasticity, cornification disorders, and dry, unkempt hair coats. Poor-quality water sources can also lead to internal organ malfunctions that can manifest outwardly as dermatopathies.

Fresh, clean water is essential to a healthy skin and coat.

Keep plenty of fresh water available to your pet at all times. Consider offering filtered or bottled water for exactly the same reasons we drink it. ("You'll either filter your water before you drink it, or force your kidneys to do so after the fact.") Also, make sure to change the water supply daily and thoroughly clean out the water bowl at least once a week.

To summarize, millions of dollars have been plowed into pet food research over the last decade, resulting in a marked increase of high-quality pet food products on the store shelves. As a result, you as a pet owner have the seemingly daunting task of choosing which one is best for your pet. You don't have to make the decision alone. Ask your veterinarian for his/her recommendation, especially if your pet is prone to skin challenges. Just remember that by feeding a high-quality diet designed specifically for your pet's individual needs, and by keeping plenty of fresh, filtered water available at all times, you can rest assured that your four-legged loved one is getting the proper nutrition necessary to keep its skin and hair coat healthy.

Chapter Four

Basic Home Grooming Techniques

A Word About Safety

Grooming should be a pleasant and safe experience, both for you and your pet. The last thing you want is a rambunctious animal hindering your efforts, thereby endangering itself and you. This is why it is imperative that dogs and cats be taught at an early age to accept grooming as part of their normal routine and to behave properly during grooming sessions. If a pet objects to any type of handling, it could be because of the following:

• Lack of desensitization and/or obedience (command) training
• Fear of the procedure
• Pain associated with the procedure

Desensitization training and obedience training should be started as early as eight weeks of age. Because this is the time in pets' lives when true memory begins, it is one of the easiest times to train them; the first things they learn tend to stick with them for a lifetime.

Proper training will help invoke a mutual respect between you and your pet that will aid your grooming efforts.

Desensitization training will condition your pet to allow its feet, ears, and mouth region to be handled without a struggle. This is vitally important for your pet's grooming program, as such permission afforded to you will allow you to trim nails, clean ears, and brush your pet's teeth without a fight.

Such training is accomplished by touching and handling these regions whenever you interact with your new puppy or kitten. Don't attempt to actually trim the nails, brush the teeth, or clean the ears; instead, pretend you are doing it. If a serious struggle ensues, stop temporarily, then resume your efforts later when your pet has calmed down. Soon, your pet will become accustomed to such handling, making future grooming efforts much easier.

As far as obedience (command) training is concerned, invest in a good book on the subject, such as *Civilizing Your Puppy,* by Barbara Wrede (Barron's, 1997). Doing so will save you a lot of headaches in the future. For grooming purposes, your dog should be well versed in the meaning of the commands *stay, sit,* and *down.* Any number of differ-

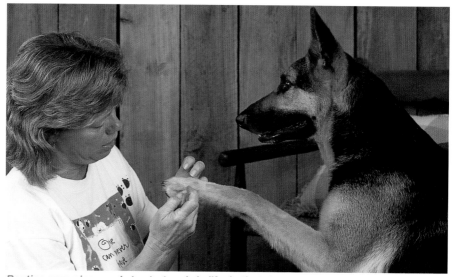

Routine grooming needs to start early in life. In that way, your pet will always be easy to handle, even if he grows large enough to argue the point.

ent training techniques can be used; just remember to keep the initial training sessions short and avoid the use of physical punishment. Physical punishment, especially on young puppies, can cause permanent behavioral problems that usually worsen as they mature. Instead of punishing for a mistake, use lots, and I mean lots, of praise (and the occasional food tidbit) for a job well done. It's been proved that pups respond favorably to this, ensuring quicker and more satisfactory training results.

As far as cats are concerned, obedience training is a bit more challenging, yet not impossible. Again, there are books available that go into the various and sometimes subtle aspects of feline obedience training, and I encourage you to get one.

Fear can play a role in problem behaviors that may arise during grooming. A good example of this is the cat that fears running water. Though you may not be able to eliminate such fears completely, you can certainly take steps to lessen them. For instance, fill that tub with water first, before bringing your pet into the room. Also, turn on the clippers well away from the pet and let it get used to the sound before actually clipping. One of the best ways to avoid "fear syndromes" is to introduce grooming procedures and grooming utensils to your pet at an early age, preferably no later than 12 weeks. Above all, make sure these first experiences are nothing but positive.

Keep the initial grooming sessions short, and allow your pet to investigate and become accus-

To apply a muzzle made from roll gauze, start with a strip of gauze positioned below the jaw; tie a knot over the bridge of the nose; bring the ends of the gauze down below the jaw and cross the ends; pull the ends behind the neck and tie in a knot. The muzzle should be applied firmly, but not too tight.

tomed to the equipment you are using beforehand. Once again, give lots of praise and offer food treats for good behavior.

Finally, pain will turn even the most obedient, easygoing Dr. Jekyll into a snapping and scratching Mr. Hyde. If you are using the correct instruments and methods, pain should rarely be a component of your grooming program. However, even with the right instruments and methods, it sometimes becomes a factor, especially if inflammation or infection is present. If a procedure is going to be painful to your pet, do not proceed with it! This is a job for your veterinarian.

In summary: Use common sense when it comes to safety and use proper restraint when needed. If your pet starts to threaten you with teeth or nails, regardless of reason, stop what you are doing immediately. Again, in these cases, let your veterinarian or professional groomer perform those procedures over which your pet absolutely throws a fit. Not only will this prevent injuries, but it will spare both you and your reluctant pet much mental anguish, despair, and alienation.

Shown here are two humane, effective methods of feline restraint.

Equipment and Supplies

To make your job easier, equip yourself with the right type of grooming tools and products. Don't be afraid to spend a little extra money for high-quality equipment; it will make the job much easier. You must be sure, however, that the tools or products you choose match your pet's particular needs. The following list includes some of the essentials that could go into a typical home grooming kit.

Brush
Comb
Scissors (blunt-tipped)
Grooming shears
Clippers (electric or cordless)
Nail trimmers
Styptic (blood-clotting) powder or
 gel
Ear cleanser-dryer
Protective eye ointment
Toothbrush/dentifrice
Cotton balls/swabs
Hypoallergenic/oatmeal shampoo
Flea and tick control products
Coat conditioner/moisturizer
Towels/blow-dryer

These grooming supplies should be easy to find. Sources include eBay, pet supply stores (brick and mortar, as well as mail-order and Internet companies), pet shops, grooming salons, department stores,

A wide variety of grooming tools is available for home pet grooming. When purchasing grooming tools, select those of good quality that will last. Shown (from left) are a nail clipper, two bristle brushes, a slicker brush, an all-purpose comb, and a flea comb.

veterinary offices, dog shows, and cat shows. Also, check your favorite dog or cat magazine for advertisements offering supplies at a discount.

One piece of equipment not mentioned in the above list is a grooming table. Professional grooming tables can be purchased that afford excellent control and comfort for the groomer and pet alike. For the home groomer on a limited budget, any table or shelf will suffice (even the floor will do!) just as long as it does not have a slippery surface. If it does, you can easily make the surface non-slip by placing a rubber bath mat on top of it. Covering the surface in some manner will also prevent it from getting scratched by toenails. Ideally, the grooming surface should be elevated high enough to allow you to perform your procedures comfortably without having to do too much bending. Your back will thank you for it!

Brushes

It's incredible how many different types of brushes you have to choose from for your pet. It is essential that you choose the right one, because inappropriate brushes could actually damage your pet's coat. Use the table on page 22 to help you make the right choice.

Bristle brushes come in a variety of shapes and textures and can be used on all types of coats. Generally speaking, the longer the hair coat, the more widely spaced and longer the bristles on the brush should be. In addition, the coarser the coat, the stiffer those bristles need to be. For example, a cat with long, silky hair would benefit most from a soft-bristled brush with bristles that are moderately to widely spaced. Conversely, a wire-haired terrier with short, coarse hair would require a stiff-bristled brush with the bristles spaced closely together.

Many groomers favor wire-pin brushes for use on dogs with medium to long hair, or on those with woolly or curly coats. Long-haired cats can also benefit from this type of brush, but some cats object to its use. As with any brush, it should be applied using full, gentle strokes to prevent breaking or damaging the hair.

Slicker brushes contain numerous fine wire bristles that are usually embedded within a square or rectangular backing. These are especially useful in removing snarls, tangles,

Recommendations for Brushing

Type of Hair Coat	Type of Brush	Direction of Brushing
Short, smooth coats (most retrievers, hounds, Chihuahuas, etc.; short-haired cats)	Soft to medium bristle brush with short, closely spaced bristles	With the grain of the coat
Short, wiry coats (terriers, etc.)	Firm bristle brush with short, closely spaced bristles; slicker brush	With the grain of the coat
Medium to long, flowing coats (Golden Retrievers, Lhasa Apso, spaniels, setters, etc.; long-haired cats)	Soft to medium bristle brush with long, medium to wide-spaced bristles; wire pin brush; slicker brush for mats and tangles	With the grain of the coat
Harsh outer coats with soft, woolly undercoats (Sheepdog, Collies, shepherds, Chow Chows, Pomeranians, etc.)	Firm bristle brush with long, wide-spaced bristles; wire pin brush; slicker brush for tangles and mats	Outer coat—with the grain; Undercoat—against the grain
Thin, delicate coats (Yorkshire Terrier, Maltese)	Wire pin brush; soft slicker brush for tangles and mats	Gentle, delicate strokes with and against the grain to prevent damage to the coat

Be sure to select the correct brush for your pet's hair coat.

and mats, as well as dense, shed undercoats. Some groomers even use slicker brushes for fluff-drying (see "Drying," page 49).

For general care and upkeep of your brush, regardless of the type, remove the hair that has accumulated on its surface after each brushing. Get a new brush if bristles are missing, or if it doesn't seem to be doing the job anymore. It's also a good idea to disinfect the brush every so often with a safe germicidal product (available from your local pet supply store). Be sure to rinse the brush off thoroughly before using again.

Combs

Like brushes, combs come in a number of sizes and shapes, each designed for a specific type of coat. The amount of space between the teeth determines which comb should be used on which coat. For example, combs with fine teeth spaced closely together are useful for dogs with short coats and for short- and long-haired cats; the wide-toothed combs are better for dogs with medium to long hair. Special combs, such as stripping combs, are useful for removing or "stripping" dead hair from the longer coats; rubber curry combs are effective at massaging the skin and removing dead hair from short-haired breeds. Rakes are specialized combs equipped with single rows of metal teeth arranged at a right angle to their handles. These combs are especially helpful for removing heavy mats and tangles.

Regardless of the type used, follow these guidelines when combing:

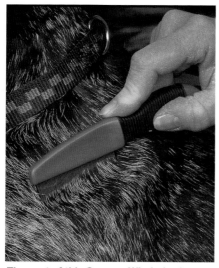

The coat of this German Wirehaired Pointer is being groomed with a flea comb. The closely spaced teeth of this handy tool is especially helpful in removing hard-to-spot parasites or debris.

- Use a comb only after you've given your pet a thorough brushing.
- To gain full benefits when using a comb, always insert the comb to its full depth into the coat.
- Never force a comb through hair. To do so could severely damage a hair coat, not to mention the discomfort it would cause your pet.
- Replace all combs that have broken or missing teeth.

Scissors/Shears

A pair of scissors, preferably blunt-tipped, can be helpful in removing loosely adhered mats and foreign objects from the coat. If you are planning to do some cosmetic grooming, you'll also need a good pair of grooming shears. Shears will give the coat a smoother cut than regular scissors will. Care and upkeep of your scissors and shears consist of cleaning them after each use and keeping them sharpened to provide the most precise cut possible.

Clippers

If you want to get into more advanced cosmetic grooming techniques, you will need to purchase a good pair of clippers (you may want to get a set anyway, because these can come in quite handy for removing mats). Oster Model A5 clippers are an excellent choice for home grooming purposes. Oster clipper blades come in different sizes for specialized uses. The table on page 70 explains the differences between these blades in greater detail. For basic home grooming techniques, the #10 and the #40 blade are satisfactory for most tasks. The #10 can be used to remove most mats and to perform minor trimming, whereas the #40, which clips all the way down to the skin, may be needed for tough mats or for clipping and exposing skin lesions or infections. If you plan to perform advanced clipping procedures, such as those presented in the section titled "Advanced Cosmetic Grooming Techniques," page 54, you will need other blades as well. Refer to that section for more details.

Because a set of high-quality clippers and blades is not cheap, you will want to be sure to take good care of them. After each use, the blades should be washed, disassembled, and oiled using blade

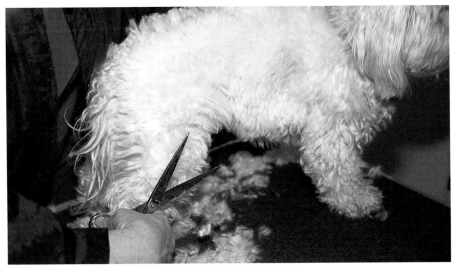

A quality pair of grooming shears can make your job easier.

wash, lubricating oil, and spray disinfectant. Follow the manufacturer's instructions concerning cleaning and blade disassembly. During use, stop periodically to brush away hair and debris that may have accumulated on the exposed blade and clipper surfaces. Also, to prevent clipper burn, be sure to keep the blades well lubricated and cool during use by using any one of the many commercially available aerosol products designed for such purposes.

If you notice any teeth missing from your clipper blades, it's time for new ones. Damaged blades can scratch or lacerate the skin surface and predispose it to infection. Similarly, dull blades can cause clipper burn by pulling hair from the hair follicles instead of neatly cutting it. Dull blades should be either replaced or sharpened before using again.

As far as the clipper assembly itself, little maintenance is usually required. Oiling, greasing, and brush

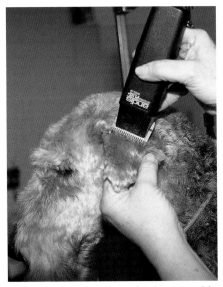

Always use sharp clipper blades to avoid giving your pet razor burn.

The guillotine-type nail clipper is the most popular for use in dog grooming.

replacement may become necessary at times. Refer to your owner's manual for more details. Finally, if you own electric clippers instead of the cordless variety, never operate them around water or on a wet hair coat. To do so could put you and your pet in danger.

Nail Accessories

Nail accessories include a good pair of toenail trimmers, and some styptic gel or powder—just in case! There are many types of nail trimmers to choose from, including guillotine trimmers, scissor or plier trimmers, and, of course, the old-fashioned human nail clippers. The latter should be reserved for only very small dogs, puppies, and kittens, whereas the other types will work on just about any size animal. Avoid using the human nail clippers on the nails of adult cats, for these

could splinter or shatter the nail. Regardless of the type used, always be sure that the blade surfaces remain sharp to avoid pulling or twisting the nail. One advantage that the guillotine trimmer has over the others is that its blade can be replaced inexpensively when dull.

Ear Cleansers and Drying Agents

As you will see later, ear cleansers and drying agents are a must for all pet owners. Pet ear cleansers come in a variety of types and ingredients. A good one should clean the ear by dissolving and emulsifying the excess wax and debris within the canal, and should dry the ear canal at the same time. This product can be obtained from your veterinarian or pet supply store.

Ophthalmic Ointment or Drops

Whenever you bathe dogs and cats, always protect their eyes before doing so. Even those products touting "no tears" can severely burn the surface of the eyes if present in strong enough concentrations. Before bathing, apply a thin strip of sterile ophthalmic ointment to each eye, then close the lids to spread the ointment evenly over the eye surfaces. You can obtain one of these sterile ointments from a pet supply store or from your veterinarian.

Dental Accessories

To help your pet maintain clean teeth and fresh breath, equip yourself with a soft-bristled toothbrush (any style will do) and a specially formulated pet dentifrice. Before you laugh at the thought of brushing your pet's teeth, just think of what your teeth would be like if you never brushed them! Clean teeth are very important in relation to your pet's overall health (see "Dental Care," page 38). Pet dentifrices come in either a paste or liquid form. These can be found just about anywhere pet supplies are sold, and are the preferred choices over such old standbys as baking soda and human toothpastes. Human preparations should be avoided if at all possible, because these can upset your pet's stomach if swallowed.

You may have seen manual dental sealers in pet stores or heard of pet owners using these instruments at home to scrape the tartar off their pets' teeth. I highly discourage such use for two reasons. First, these instruments are rarely effective at removing tartar where it really counts—up under the gum line. Trying to perform the procedure on a nonsedated dog or cat can lead to severe injury to yourself or your pet. Second, if you scale the teeth without also polishing them afterward, you are defeating the purpose. Scaling creates little nicks and etches in the tooth enamel that, unless polished smooth again, will act as a site for plaque and tartar buildup, this time even faster than before.

Cotton Balls and Swabs

Keep plenty of cotton balls and swabs handy to clean around the eyes and ears. Cotton balls can be placed in the outer ears before bathing to keep out moisture. Never stick anything deep into the ear canal, especially cotton swabs. This probing will push debris farther down into the ear and can do great damage to the eardrum.

Shampoos

The three most common grooming errors that pet owners commit with regard to shampoos for their pets are
• using a shampoo formulated for human use,
• using a medicated shampoo without having the pet's skin condition diagnosed by a veterinarian, and
• using dog shampoos on cats.

Remember: Bathing is necessary only if the skin and coat are dirty or if a medical condition exists. In fact, frequent brushing and combing are probably the most important things you can do to keep your pet clean. However, if a cleanup bath is indicated, there are many excellent cleansing shampoos available that will do the job gently and effectively. The brand you use isn't as important as the formulation (although many do a better job than others). Avoid human shampoos and preparations because these can be too acidic for your dog's or cat's skin, and often do more harm than good. Instead, look for one that is formulated especially for dogs and cats. If your pet likes to roll around in the flower bed and you are having to resort to the bath one or more times weekly, consider

Active Ingredients of Medicated Shampoos and/or Conditioners

Ingredient	Used to Treat	Comments
Coal tar	Seborrhea, itching, skin inflammation	Can be toxic to cats unless highly refined; unpleasant odor
Sulfur	Seborrhea, bacterial infection, itching, skin inflammation	Unpleasant odor; often combined with coal tar for synergistic effect
Selenium	Seborrhea, skin infections, itching	—
Salicylic acid	Skin inflammation	Active ingredient of aspirin; should not be used on cats
Benzoyl peroxide	Folliculitis, seborrhea, itching, demodectic mange (as support treatment)	Can be irritating to the skin; may bleach colored fabrics and clothing
Chlorhexidine	Bacterial and fungal skin infections	Effective against ringworm; safe for cats
Triclosan	Bacterial skin infections	—
Povidone iodine	Bacterial and fungal skin infections	Effective against ringworm; use with caution in cats
Miconazole	Ringworm and other fungal skin infections; *Malassezia* dermatitis	—
Pramoxine HCl	Itching, seborrhea	Often used with colloidal oatmeal in conditioners
Colloidal oatmeal	Dry, irritated skin, itching	Has good anti-inflammatory effects
Chitosanide	Dry, irritated skin	Creates a protective film on the skin surface, helping to seal in moisture
Lanolin, oils, fatty alcohols, glycerol esters	Dry, irritated skin	Soften and soothe the skin
Propylene glycol, urea, glycerin	Dry, irritated skin	Add moisture to the skin
Aloe vera	Irritated, inflamed skin	Reduce discomfort caused by skin inflammation
Aluminum acetate, silver nitrate, tannic acid	Moist dermatitis	Used as adjunct treatment for hot spots inflammation

refining your choice even more by using a soap-free hypoallergenic shampoo. There are many good ones on the market to choose from, and your veterinarian will be able to recommend one for you. Select a shampoo that contains plenty of moisturizers and conditioners. Alternatively, you can apply a moisturizer during the rinse or after bathing.

If your dog or cat has a white coat, consider using a shampoo that contains a bluing agent (this will usually be indicated on the label). Bluing is also available at your grocery store and can be added directly to the rinse water. The result of either method will be a whiter, brighter coat.

If your pet has a skin condition and you believe a medicated shampoo might help, the first step is to consult your veterinarian. You should use a medicated shampoo only under the supervision of your veterinarian. Despite good intentions, blindly selecting a medicated shampoo when you are not familiar with the chemical involved could adversely affect your pet. The table on page 28 lists the ingredients commonly found in many of the medicated shampoos prescribed for dogs and cats, and their indications.

Coat Conditioners, Moisturizers, and Emollients

Skin and coat conditioners are designed to lubricate skin surfaces and to help prevent tangles and mats from forming within the coat. They also help replace the natural oils lost from the skin and hair because of bathing and disease. These oils act as moisturizers by helping to retain moisture next to the skin, thereby leaving the skin and coat soft and supple. Emollients are substances that soothe and soften the skin surface. They have been proved to be helpful if the skin is especially sensitive or irritated. Most after-bath products found at a pet store contain a combination of conditioners, moisturizers, and/or emollients. For best results, choose a rinse for after bathing (when the skin is still moist), and a spray for between baths. Note, however, that if your pet has a skin disorder, such as a moist hot spot, you should consult your veterinarian before using any after-bath product (see "Hot Spots," page 90).

Specific Techniques

Giving Your Pet an At-Home Physical Examination

As mentioned previously, grooming sessions provide the ideal opportunity to assess the health status of your pet. Mini-examinations are quick and easy to perform, and can be very effective in the early detection of health problems, before they become well established. Examine your pet at least once a week, using the checklist provided on page 30 as a guide. An abnormal finding should prompt you to contact your veterinarian to obtain a

The Physical Exam

General Evaluation

- [ ] Alert
- [ ] Active
- [ ] Good appetite

- [ ] Abnormal posture
- [ ] Lameness*
- [ ] Weak*

- [ ] Lethargic*
- [ ] Poor appetite*
- [ ] Weight loss/gain*

Skin and Hair Coat

- [ ] Appear normal
- [ ] Hair loss
- [ ] Dull
- [ ] Scaly
- [ ] Dry

- [ ] Oily
- [ ] Itching
- [ ] Shedding
- [ ] Mats
- [ ] Tumors or warts

- [ ] Infection
- [ ] Abnormal lumps
- [ ] Foreign matter
- [ ] Parasites

Eyes

- [ ] Appear normal
- [ ] Discharge
- [ ] Redness

- [ ] Eyelid abnormalities
- [ ] Squinting
- [ ] Infection

- [ ] Unequal pupils
- [ ] Cloudiness
- [ ] Discoloration

Ears

- [ ] Appear normal
- [ ] Inflamed
- [ ] Itchy
- [ ] Discharge

- [ ] Head shaking
- [ ] Parasites
- [ ] Bad odor
- [ ] Tumors

- [ ] Excessive hair
- [ ] Head tilt

Nose and Throat

- [ ] Appear normal
- [ ] Nasal discharge

- [ ] Enlarged lymph nodes
- [ ] Dry, crusty nose

Mouth, Teeth, and Gums

- [ ] Appear normal
- [ ] Broken teeth
- [ ] Retained baby teeth
- [ ] Tartar build-up

- [ ] Tumors
- [ ] Loose teeth
- [ ] Gingivitis
- [ ] Excess salivation

- [ ] Pale gums
- [ ] Ulcers

Miscellaneous

- [ ] Tense/painful abdomen
- [ ] Coughing/wheezing
- [ ] Abnormal stools

- [ ] Abnormal urination
- [ ] Abnormal water consumption
- [ ] Genital discharge

- [ ] Mammary lumps
- [ ] Scooting

* = abnormal

professional evaluation. Also remember that these home examinations are no substitute for routine veterinary checkups, which should be performed at least once a year.

Ear Care

Approximately 7 out of 10 dogs and cats seen by veterinarians have dirty ears. Many of these pets also have infections brewing in those ears. For this reason, preventive ear care for all dogs and cats is essential. By keeping the ears clean and dry, you can thwart potential problems right from the start, before they become chronic.

Let's begin by reviewing some basic anatomical features of the canine and feline ear. The ear flaps, or *pinnae,* are those structures that surround the opening into the ear. They come in a number of styles, ranging from short, pointy ones to the long, droopy variety. The external ear opening leads into the initial steep portion of the ear canal, termed the *vertical canal,* which soon bends horizontally to form the *horizontal ear canal.* This is where most waxy debris and moisture tend to build up, because the bend in the ear canal effectively traps it there. The eardrum, or *tympanic membrane,* lies at the end of the horizontal canal and marks the entrance into the middle ear. The inner ear, which contains the nerve endings responsible for the sense of hearing, communicates directly with this middle ear canal. Ear wax, called *cerumen,* is produced by glands lining the ear canals and forms a thin,

Dogs with erect ears tend to have less ear challenges than their floppy-eared peers do.

protective barrier that maintains a constant and healthy environment within the ear. Complications arise when too much wax is produced. This can be caused by inflammation, excessive moisture and/or heat, parasites, allergies, or any other condition that threatens to disrupt the "normal environment" and pave the way toward infection. Excessive ear wax can act as an ideal growth medium for yeast and bacteria.

Signs of an ear disorder usually are easily recognized. A constant shaking of the head and scratching at the ears are sure signals that something is wrong with one or both ears. The problem may be an infection, a foreign body (such as grass awns), parasites (such as ticks and ear mites), or simply an excess accumulation of hair within the ear canal. Brown to black discharges from the ears are commonly seen with ear mites or yeast infections; yellow, creamy discharges indicate that a bacterial infection is likely to be present. More serious symptoms, such as tilting the head or circling to one side, can appear as an infection spreads into the middle ear through a diseased or ruptured eardrum. In these cases, permanent hearing damage can result if vigorous treatment is not instituted immediately.

There is another condition worth special mention that can affect the ears of dogs and cats: aural hematomas. Aural hematomas are soft, fluid-filled swellings that can suddenly appear on the inner surfaces of one or both pinnae. These swellings are believed to result from fractures involving the cartilage within the ear, leading to an accumulation of blood and serum in the space between the skin and the cartilage itself. Allergies and ear infections are both believed to be the most com-

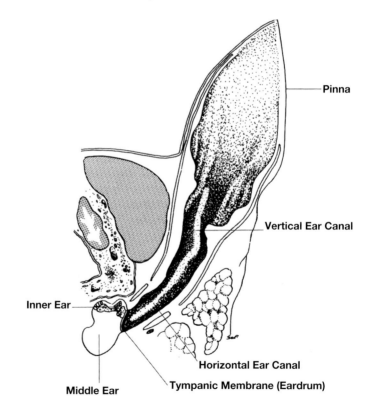

The Canine Ear.

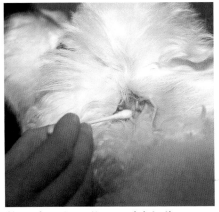

Never insert a cotton swab into the ear canal itself.

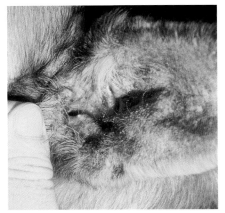

Bacterial infection of the ear (otitis externa).

mon causes of aural hematomas, as these conditions can lead to excessive head shaking and scratching that can damage the ear cartilage.

Simply draining the fluid from the ear flap with a needle and syringe provides only a temporary fix, and could introduce bacteria into the site, leading to a nasty secondary infection. As a result, surgical intervention, involving drainage followed by a surgical "tack down" of the skin to the damaged cartilage, is the only effective way to treat and to prevent recurrences of aural hematomas.

See your veterinarian right away if you suspect any type of ear problem in your dog or cat. An early, proper diagnosis is essential for effective treatment because this determines which medication or treatment is required. Needless to say, even the most minor infections can quickly become serious if not treated correctly. Furthermore, sometimes an ear disorder is merely the outward sign of a more serious disease, such as hypothyroidism or an immune deficiency. At the first sign of a problem seek help from a professional.

Now that we've seen some of the maladies that can affect the ear, let's turn our attention to preventing ear infections. Preventive ear care is not difficult; basically, all that is involved is the use of an ear cleanser/drying agent and, if needed, a periodic ear pluck.

An ear pluck is necessary if there is visible hair blocking the opening of the ear canal. Many pet owners take it upon themselves to perform this task, but there are two reasons why this procedure should be left to a veterinarian. First, ear plucking can be a painful experience for your pet. And pain is a major factor that causes a pet to misbehave during a grooming session (see "A Word About Safety," page 17). As a result, this procedure has a high incidence of serious bite wounds being

Inspect your pet's ears regularly for any redness and/or discharge.

inflicted upon owners. The second reason for letting your veterinarian perform ear plucks is that whenever hair is forcibly removed from its follicle, inflammation occurs within that follicle. This can lead to a bad ear infection if medications are not instilled in the ears after plucking or if an actual medicated ear flush is not performed. If this is not done, you risk doing more harm with the ear pluck than good. Let your veterinarian perform this procedure.

The ears should be cleaned and dried at least twice a month, as well as after bathing, swimming, or any other contact with water. Use a general-purpose ear cleanser available from your veterinarian or from your favorite pet supply store. Liquids are more desirable than powders, because powders can actually become storehouses for moisture once they've become saturated. Although it may seem a contradiction to apply a liquid into an area you

are trying to keep dry, these preparations contain drying agents (astringents); that which remains within the ear after application will actually help create a moisture-reduced environment. To clean the ears, first gently pull the ear flap out toward you (not upward!) to straighten the vertical ear canal. Next, instill some of the cleaning solution into each ear and massage the ears well for 15 to 20 seconds. Afterward, release the flap and stand back: an immediate head shake should follow, and you may be surprised at what comes out of those ears! Once complete, take a tissue, cotton ball, or cotton swab and remove any visible wax or debris from the inside of the pinna and outermost portions of the ear canal. Again, never insert anything down into the ear canal, except for the cleansing solution. If using cotton swabs, you should never lose sight of the cotton tip during the cleaning process.

One further word of caution. If your pet is showing any of the signs of ear disease mentioned above, consult your veterinarian before putting anything into the ear. If the eardrum is ruptured or has a hole in it because of its diseased nature, there is the danger of an improper medication seeping into the middle ear, causing serious complications.

Eye Care

Eye care is a vital part of any grooming program, owing to the role that these organs play. Special care is required to guard against inadvertent injury to the eyes when performing such grooming procedures as bathing and clipping. But just as important, pet owners must train themselves to recognize subtle signs that may indicate a problem involving the eyes. Inspections should be made routinely, for the sooner an abnormal condition is detected, the better the chances are for favorable treatment.

The actual eyeball, or globe, is composed of many structures, all of which work in unison toward a common goal: the creation and perception of a visual image. The outer surface of the eye consists of the *cornea, sclera,* and *conjunctival membrane.* The cornea is the translucent structure covering the outer front portion of the globe. Composed of several layers of epithelial cells, the cornea is responsible for gathering light and directing it along the proper path to be processed. The sclera is that portion of the eye better known as the "white" of the eye. Although it serves no particular function as far as vision is concerned, an abnormal sclera color could mean that your pet is suffering from some underlying disease condition. For instance, a yellow scleral color indicates an underlying liver or blood disorder, whereas a red scleral color can result from trauma, high blood pressure, or pressure shifts within the eyes.

Finally, the conjunctival membrane is a thin layer of tissue covering part of the sclera, as well as the inner portions of the eyelids. *Conjunctivitis* is a term you may have heard of; it is simply used to describe an inflammation involving this structure.

Once light passes through the clear cornea, it proceeds into the inner portions of the eye through the pupil, the black hole that is surrounded by the colored structure called the iris. As light passes through the pupil, it proceeds through the fens, which then focuses the image on the retina, on the posterior inner surface of the eyeball. The retina, which is composed of cells and numerous tiny nerve endings, in turn transmits these messages to the brain, which ultimately translates them into the conscious perception of the image.

The eyelids of both dogs and cats function to spread the tear film secreted by the lacrimal glands over the surface of the eyes, and to protect the globes from trauma or foreign matter. Because they serve these vital needs, any disruptions or abnormalities in the normal anatomy

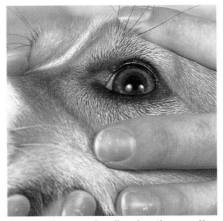

Inspect the eyes for discolorations and/or discharges.

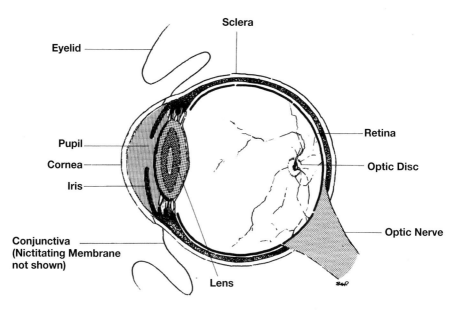

Eyelid

Sclera

Pupil

Cornea

Iris

Retina

Optic Disc

Optic Nerve

Conjunctiva
(Nictitating Membrane
not shown)

Lens

The Eye.

of the eyelids, such as tumors or ingrown eyelashes, could prove disastrous to the eyes themselves if not corrected quickly.

Besides conventional eyelids, dogs and cats have third eyelids, called *nictitating membranes,* at the inner corner of each eye. Not only are they protective in nature, but they are also thought to produce some of the normal tear film. Protrusion of these structures over the surfaces of the globes may be a sign of disease, and should prompt you to seek medical attention for your pet at once.

When performing your mini-examination on your pet (see "Giving Your Pet an At-Home Physical Examination," page 29), look closely at the eyes and the lids. If you detect any abnormalities, regardless of how

trivial they may seem, consult your veterinarian.

Whenever you bathe your pet, you should apply protection to the outer surfaces of the eyes to prevent irritation from soap. The corneas of dogs and cats are very sensitive to foreign matter and to chemicals, and may be injured easily. Even products touted as "tearless" can do significant harm if they come in contact with the corneas of dogs and cats. As mentioned previously, a sterile ophthalmic ointment is the preferred protective substance to be applied to the eyes (see "Ophthalmic Ointment or Drops," page 26). Your veterinarian should carry such ointment or, if not, can obtain it for you. When applying the ointment, be sure to keep the nozzle of the tube parallel

Tear stains can be a persistent problem and are most unsightly with longhaired, light-colored pets.

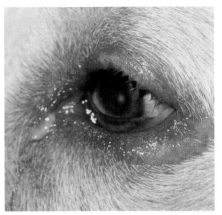

Eye infections require prompt medical attention.

to the eye surface. In this way, there is less chance of injuring the eye if your pet should move suddenly.

Excessively long hair that touches the eyes will cause unsightly eye discharges, conjunctival infections, and, in severe cases, corneal damage. As a preventive measure, be sure to trim away any hair that hangs close to the eyes. Use only blunt-nose scissors when working around the eyes, always keeping them parallel to the edge of the eyelid and covering the eyes with your hand as you trim.

"Tear staining" is a troublesome phenomenon seen in certain breeds of dogs, such as Poodles, and even in some cats. It usually shows up as a brownish discoloration of the hair under the eyes next to the bridge of the nose. Caused by chronic inflammation and/or infection involving the tear-producing structures of the eyelids, this condition is not serious and poses no significant health hazards to those pets involved.

If your pet is troubled with tear-staining, you can take certain measures to help lessen its effect. For instance, you can wipe the affected regions on a daily basis using a dilute hydrogen peroxide (1:10) solution—being very careful to keep this solution out of the eyes. In addition, petroleum jelly applied to the corners of both eyes where the staining occurs will help divert tear flow from these regions and reduce staining. Many commercial products are also available to help get rid of or mask existing discoloration.

To prevent infection caused by moisture buildup on the skin in the affected areas, agents used to clean and dry the ears can be used to promote dryness (see "Ear Cleansers and Drying Agents," page 26). Again, regardless of what is used, remember that you are working around the eyes. Use care to avoid the eye surfaces when applying any of these products.

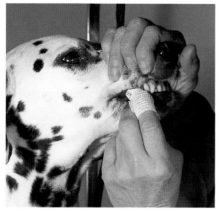

Focus on the outer gum line when brushing the teeth.

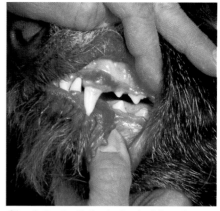

Check the teeth for tartar buildup along the gum line.

Dental Care

The teeth of dogs and cats require just as much routine preventive at-home care as the skin and coat do. Only recently have veterinarians and pet owners alike concentrated on the benefits afforded by keeping the teeth free of plaque and tartar.

Now for a brief anatomy lesson: Each tooth consists of a crown, that portion above the gum line covered by tough enamel; a neck at the gum line; and the root(s), that portion below the gum that is imbedded in bone. Adult dogs have a complement of 42 permanent teeth, whereas cats have 30. Aside from the total number of teeth, the anatomy and physiology (and dental care) are the same, regardless of species.

Periodontal disease is characterized by the buildup of plaque and tartar on the teeth above and below

the gum line; this in turn leads to gum inflammation and tooth loss. This affliction is one of the most prevalent health disorders affecting dogs and cats today. Well over 80 percent of all dogs and cats show some indications of this disease by the time they are just three years of age. To make matters worse, dirty teeth and infected gums can seed the bloodstream with bacteria, causing heart valve infections and/or kidney disease in pets.

You might ask, "But what about hard food or biscuits? Aren't these supposed to keep the teeth clean?" Although it is true that the scraping action caused by chewing these hard items does help remove some tartar, the actual amounts removed are rarely satisfactory to prevent periodontal disease. In addition, in dogs and cats (as in people), these starchy foodstuffs can actually promote tartar buildup and bacterial

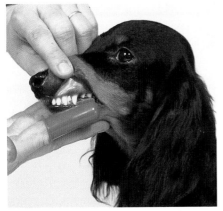

A finger brush is an excellent tool for brushing your pet's teeth.

The incisor teeth of small dog breeds are especially prone to periodontal disease.

growth on the teeth. As a result, using these food items as your pet's sole means of dental care may give you a false sense of security.

If dental tartar is already visible at the gum line, you will need to have your pet's teeth professionally cleaned by your veterinarian. He or she will use an ultrasonic dental sealer to break apart and remove the hard tartar deposits above and below the gum line. Afterwards, the teeth will be polished to restore a smooth surface to the crowns of the teeth.

Once professional cleaning has been performed, routine at-home dental care should be started using specially formulated pet dentifrices (see "Dental Accessories," page 26). The paste or solution that you ultimately choose can be applied using a toothbrush, a soft cloth, or even your fingers. Brush as you would your own teeth. Concentrate your efforts along the gum line and outer surfaces of the teeth. Rinsing is unnecessary.

Brushing the teeth on a daily basis would be ideal; at a minimum, cleanse them at least twice weekly. Many cats and dogs refuse to let their owners near their mouths. If this

Cleaning your pet's teeth is easier if you begin early in his or her life.

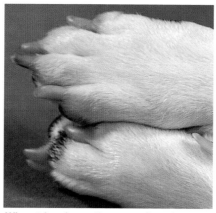

When trimming nails, remember also to shorten the dewclaws.

is the case with your pet, don't press the issue. Obviously, you don't want to get bitten in the process. All pets should receive a yearly dental

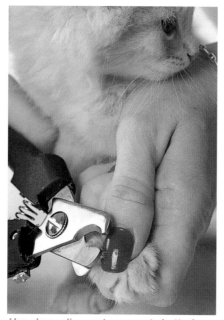

Use sharp clippers to prevent shattering your cat's nails.

checkup by your veterinarian and a professional cleaning when needed.

Nail Care

It is very important to check your pet's nails on a regular basis to see if they need trimming. Long nails get snagged and torn easily, and also place undue stress upon the joints of the paws. When a dog's paw is resting flat on the floor, the ends of the nails should not be bearing any weight. If they are, they are too long. Also remember to trim the dewclaws. Many owners whose dogs have dewclaws forget to trim the nails attached to these appendages; this can lead to ingrown toenails and infections. If present, dewclaws can be found on the inside of the front and/or hind legs, just above the paws themselves. Dewclaws serve no useful function; they represent the vestigial first digit in dogs. With few exceptions, they are usually removed by veterinarians in the first week of life, so don't be surprised if your dog doesn't have any.

Cats don't have dewclaws per se. But, unlike dogs, they do have retractable toenails that can be called into service at a moment's notice. Even though your cat may use a scratching post (or your furniture, for that matter) to sharpen those claws, they still need periodic trimming. Feline nails tend to be more fragile than those of dogs, so use special care when clipping them.

If the nail is clear, you should be able to note the line of demarcation between the pink quick (the portion of the nail that contains the blood supply) and the rest of the nail. Using the clippers, snip off the latter portion just in front of the quick. For those pets with black or brown nails, it is slightly more difficult. Try shining a bright light (from a flashlight or penlight) on the nails before trimming to see if the demarcation can be discerned. If not, trim off small portions at a time until the nail is no longer bearing weight. On some nails, you might be able to see a little black circle in the middle of the tip. If so, start trimming the nail back, little by little. You will notice that this black ring gets bigger with each cut. When it becomes so large that it almost covers the entire end of the nail, it is time to stop.

Although you want to avoid hitting the quick, it is not the end of the world if you do so. Just apply direct pressure to the end of the bleeding nail for three to five minutes, using a tissue, cloth, or piece of gauze. You can also use styptic powder or gel to stop the blood flow.

Finally, many pets dislike having their feet and nails touched or manipulated. If this is the case with your cat or dog, don't press the issue. Your veterinarian or professional groomer will do it for a nominal fee.

Anal Sac Care

If you ever see your dog scooting its hind end along the floor, chances are it's because of anal sac irritation or impaction. These sacs, not to be confused with anal glands, are on either side of the anus, at about the eight o'clock and four o'clock positions. Each sac is lined with secretory cells and connects to the anus via a small duct. The fluid produced by these cells smells foul and can be quite irritating if allowed to remain within the sac for an appreciable amount of time. Research has shown that anal sac fluid provides a means of identification between individual animals (which explains why dogs go around sniffing each other). Normally, these sacs empty every time a bowel movement occurs; however, several factors can interrupt this normal emptying. For instance, obesity, inflammation (as seen with allergies), parasites, and diets low in fiber can all lead to anal sac impaction. When this occurs, the dog resorts to the scooting action mentioned herein, as

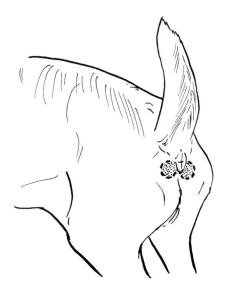

This is the normal position of the dog's anal sacs.

Different kinds of coats require different kinds of handling. The harsh coat of the Scottish Terrier needs vigorous brushing with a stiff brush.

the dog tries to facilitate their evacuation. If the impaction is not relieved, infection can result. This disorder can also be seen in cats, but the incidence of anal sac problems in felines is quite low.

A dog's anal sacs should be emptied manually only if a problem exists; this will be manifested by scooting or constant chewing or licking at the tail end. Many people advocate emptying the anal sacs on a routine basis, whether they need emptying or not. The problem with this is that squeezing and pushing on otherwise healthy sacs can cause inflammation, which can subse-

quently lead to impaction. Thus, instead of preventing a problem, you may be creating one. If expressing the anal sacs is necessary, let your groomer or veterinarian perform this procedure.

Brushing and Combing

Brushing helps remove dead hair and skin cells, prevents tangles and mats, spreads natural oils over the surface of the hair coat, and stimulates new hair growth. Performed daily, it will help maintain the coat in a clean and manageable condition.

Before starting a routine brushing session, spray a coat conditioner, moisturizer, or even plain water onto the coat and massage it in well with your hands. This will make your brushing much easier and more effective. Once you've done this, begin brushing from head to tail, using firm but gentle strokes.

For dogs with thick hair or thick undercoats, such as the Collie, Chow Chow, Norwegian Elkhound, Pomeranian, and others, brush from the skin outward against the grain or lie to remove the dead portion of the undercoat. Use a curling motion with your brush for most effective results. Once you have covered the entire coat in this fashion, go back and brush the surface hair, this time with the grain.

For all other types of coats, including those of cats, brush with the grain of the hair. For long-haired cats or those dogs with thin, silky coats (such as the Yorkshire Terrier), use long, gentle strokes to prevent

Regular brushing is vital for keeping the hair coat of the older dog bright and healthy.

tearing or damaging the hair. Conversely, short, wiry coats may require shorter, more vigorous strokes to achieve the desired effects. Your pet's attitude will be a gauge of your method. If your pet is not enjoying it, you are probably being too rough in your brushing.

A comb may now be used to loosen tangles and remove any dead hair that the brush failed to get. Use it on any long hair present on the extremities and for combing out the long hair found on the ears and face. Never use a comb on a thick undercoat unless you are using it to help remove a mat.

For removal of shed hair that may have been missed by the brush and comb, consider using a lint brush, or even a handheld portable vacuum—

assuming, of course, that your pet will consent to its use! Finally, as an added touch, a soft cloth, glove, or velvet pad rubbed over the surface of the entire coat will help "buff" it to a nice, shiny finish.

Removing Mats and Tangles

Mats and tangles are caused by repeated chewing, licking, or scratching at a particular area on an animal's hair coat. Foreign matter such as gum can also act as a site around which a tangle, and then a mat, can develop. The most common problem areas are behind the ears, on the chest, and near the tail end, although mats and tangles can occur anywhere on the body to which the pet has access. When a mat forms, it traps dirt and moisture next to the

The best way to deal with mats and tangles is to keep them from appearing to begin with.

skin and creates a perfect environment for an infection. This is compounded by the fact that the skin often becomes traumatized as the pet continues to lick and chew at the area. To avoid further problems, mats and tangles need to be removed as soon as they are noticed.

Brushing helps keep the pet's natural oils spread evenly over the coat. The result will be obvious in well-cared-for, healthy dogs.

If you find a mat while brushing your dog, work it out gently with your fingers.

Use smooth, gentle strokes when brushing.

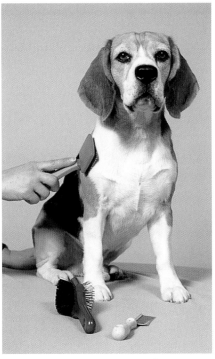

A slicker brush can be quite effective for removing tangles and shed hair in long coats and can even work well on shorter coats.

Begin by lightly moistening the mat or tangle with water or conditioner and working it free as much as possible with your fingers, comb, and/or slicker brush. If the mat is closely adhered to the skin, support its base with your fingers to prevent it from pulling on the skin. Start at the roots of the hairs and work outward. If, after much effort, you are still not successful, consider cutting out the mat or tangle with scissors or clippers. Don't worry about the lost hair; it will grow back. The main thing to remember is this: never try

to cut out a mat unless you can clearly see where the hair meets the skin. Countless pets have been wounded by owners who failed to heed this advice. To help you achieve this line of demarcation, insert a pair of scissors or forceps into the base of the mat and then open them up, bluntly separating the matted hairs as you go. After doing this a few times, you should be able to pass a pair of scissors or clippers beneath the mat and cut it free. All this takes time and patience, not only on your part but on your pet's

A shedding blade in action.

as well. If your pet is badly matted or particularly fractious during the procedure, it would be wise to seek the help of a professional groomer or veterinarian.

When you finally remove the mat or tangle, inspect the skin beneath to be sure it is not reddened or inflamed. If there appears to be a slight irritation, it should resolve now that the mat has been removed. If infection is present or the area is severely inflamed, seek veterinary medical attention immediately.

Bathing

When bath time finally arrives, consider where the bath is to take place. For smaller dogs and cats, the bathtub, laundry tub, or kitchen sink will suffice. If your pet requires a larger space—or if you simply refuse to share your tub—there are other options available. A garden hose and a bucket or empty milk container for rinsing will work fine outdoors. A plastic wading pool can also serve as a tub substitute. One word of caution: before using this, be prepared to get wet!

A number of "pre-bath" procedures need to be completed before you actually break out the shampoo. These can be done in or out of the tub or sink, whichever is more convenient for you:

1. Brush and/or comb the coat thoroughly.

2. Remove any tangles, mats, or unwanted hair that may be present (see "Removing Mats and Tangles,"

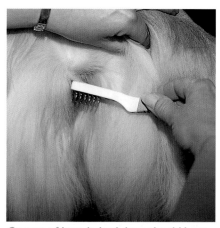
Owners of long-haired dogs should have a rake to remove mats.

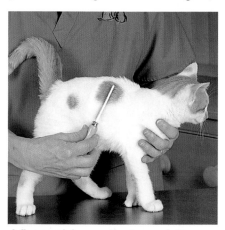
A flea comb is a gentle, appropriate grooming tool for a kitten.

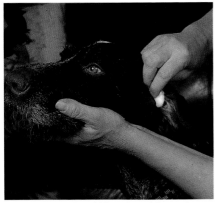

Cotton balls should be placed in each ear prior to bathing to help keep water from entering the ear canal.

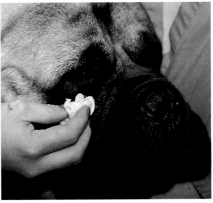

Clean any skin folds around the face prior to bathing.

page 43). Use your clippers or scissors to remove any fecal matter that may have become matted in the hair around the tail. Trim away any hair dangling in and around the eyes using blunt-tipped scissors or clippers.

3. Swab the outer ear canal and inner ear flap gently with a tissue, cotton ball, or cotton swab to remove all visible dirt and wax, then clean both ear canals using your all-purpose ear cleanser (see "Ear Care," page 31). After cleaning, insert a cotton ball into each ear to help keep bath water from entering the canals.

4. Trim the toenails, if needed, starting with the front feet and proceeding to the hind feet (see "Nail Care," page 40).

5. Apply ophthalmic ointment to the surfaces of both eyes for protection from the shampoo. Keep the edge of the tube parallel to the eyelid margins (to avoid injury if your pet moves unexpectedly) and squeeze some of the ointment onto the eye

surfaces, then manually open and close the lids to spread the ointment evenly across the corneas. If you are not sure how much to use at a time, keep in mind that it is better to use too much than too little. Be sure that the entire surfaces of the eyes are protected (see "Eye Care," page 34).

Summary of Bathing Routine for Dogs and Cats

1. Brush and/or comb thoroughly.
2. Remove all mats and tangles.
3. Clean, swab, and pack the ears.
4. Clip the toenails.
5. Apply eye ointment.
6. Bathe and rinse.
7. Squeeze excess water from the coat.
8. Towel- and/or blow-dry.
9. After (or during) drying, brush the coat thoroughly.

Once you have completed these preliminary maneuvers, you are ready to bathe your pet. If you are using the tub or sink, be sure the drain cover is

The water used for bathing and rinsing should be lukewarm.

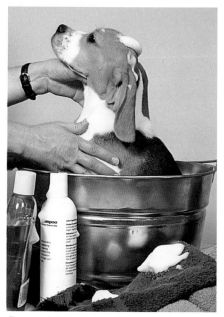

Be careful to avoid getting soap in a pet's eyes when lathering.

in place to catch the excess hair. A piece of steel wool placed over the drain will also serve this purpose. Place a towel or, better yet, a rubber bath mat on the bottom of the tub or sink to ensure ample footing. If you do this, your pet will feel much more comfortable with this often unnerving situation. Turn on the water and let it run for a few seconds to allow the temperature to stabilize. Ideally, the bath water should be lukewarm and comfortable to the touch. If it is too cold or too hot to keep your fingers immersed in it, then it is too cold or hot for the bath.

Once the water reaches the proper temperature, place your pet into the tub or sink and thoroughly soak the coat with water. Next, apply

the shampoo. If you are applying a medicated shampoo, be sure to wear protective gloves.

Using a systematic approach, start with the neck region, then wash the back, tail end, sides, belly, underarms, and legs. Massage the shampoo into the hair and down to the skin. If needed, add water for more lather. Next, take a cloth or sponge, saturate it with water and shampoo, and carefully clean around the head and face.

Now rinse completely, using the same systematic approach that was used for the shampooing. (Note: If a medicated shampoo is being used, allow at least 10 to 15 minutes of skin contact before rinsing it off.) Use fresh water for the rinse. It can be applied using a cup, milk jug, or, better yet, a sprayer hose. Double-check the armpits, groin, toes, and genitalia once you are finished to be sure these areas are shampoo-free; these regions are often missed or inadequately rinsed. It is vital that all areas be thoroughly rinsed because shampoo residue that dries in contact with the skin can cause irritation and lead to chewing and other self-induced trauma.

Ideally, a conditioner should be added to the rinse water to help moisturize the skin and create a more manageable, tangle-free coat once the bath procedure is completed (see "Coat Conditioners, Moisturizers, and Emollients," page 29). If the coat was especially dirty, a second shampoo and rinse may be needed. If so, repeat the foregoing procedures step by step.

Drying

Squeeze the excess water from the coat, then take a cotton towel and rub the hair briskly, starting from the head and working back toward the tail. Use a rubbing motion that is first directed with the grain or lie of the hair, then against the grain. Avoid circular motions when towel-drying, as this could cause tangles and mats. Once the towel you are using becomes saturated with moisture, change to another one. Keep towel-drying in this fashion until the towels no longer become saturated. To expedite the process, run a brush through the coat between towel changes. This will help prevent tan-

Be sure to rinse thoroughly after bathing.

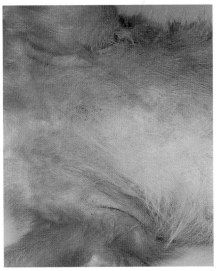

This is what can happen to the skin if shampoo is not rinsed off properly.

Dry your pet thoroughly after bathing.

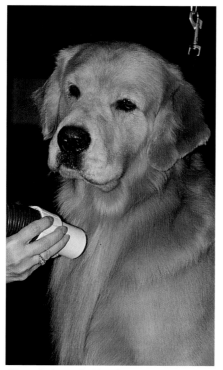

Blow-drying a Golden Retriever.

gling and remove moisture. As an alternative to towels, consider chamois cloths, similar to the ones used to dry cars. These are very effective at capturing moisture from the coat and will make the drying quicker and easier.

After towel-drying, spray on a conditioner if none was previously added to the rinse water. Brush the entire coat thoroughly to work in the conditioner and undo any tangles that may have formed during the towel-drying.

For short-coated dogs and cats, towel-drying alone should suffice. Be certain to keep your pet protected from drafts or chills until the coat is completely dry. Towel-drying is also the method of choice if your pet has sensitive skin or suffers from a skin ailment, because blow-drying and fluff-drying can aggravate these conditions. Also, some dogs and cats simply will not tolerate having a dryer turned on in their presence. If this is the case with your pet, continue with towel-drying. Remember, however, that when using a towel as the sole means of drying, you must keep your pet inside until it is completely dry. If you don't, it may search out the first patch of grass or dirt (or no telling what else) available and roll in it. Needless to say, you may find yourself back at the bathtub sooner than expected!

If your pet has longer hair or a thick undercoat, you may want to blow-dry (fluff-dry) in addition to the towel-drying. All you need for this is a dependable handheld hair dryer and a brush. The technique is basically the same as that used when you blow-dry your own hair. With the dryer setting on warm, not hot, direct the airflow onto one section of the coat and concentrate your brushing on that particular area. Direct your brush strokes against the grain or lie of the hair. The idea is to isolate and dry the hair from the inside out, starting at the moist undercoat and working out to the outer coat. Again, start at the head region and continue back toward the tail. Move from section to section, brushing and blow-drying against the grain, until the coat is completely dry. If you do not want a "fluffed" appearance to the coat, finish by going back over the outer coat with your brush, brushing with the grain of the hair.

An alternate method of drying that many professional groomers use is cage-drying. This involves placing the towel-dried, damp pet in a cage and attaching a dryer to the cage door, effectively freeing the groomer's hands to do other things. Under proper supervision, this is an effective and effortless way to dry dogs and cats. Unfortunately, it is also an impractical method for the home pet groomer to use. If this method is to be carried out properly and safely, a high-powered dryer that does not blow hot air but instead "forces" the water off the hair coat should be purchased. You must also purchase a cage large enough to allow for adequate air circulation and ventilation. Just in case you were thinking about improvising,

Towel-drying a Chow Chow puppy.

travel kennels or similar carriers are not adequate for cage-drying. These enclosures are not designed for this purpose and do not provide adequate ventilation to be used safely.

Tips for Bathing Cats

Giving a cat a bath can be a very tricky procedure, to say the least. If you own one of those rare cats that doesn't mind, or even enjoys the water and shampoo, consider yourself lucky. More often than not, it is the cat owner who actually gets the bath—with a few claw and tooth marks thrown in for good measure. If you fall into this category, consider these tips when the dreaded bath time arrives.

Fill the tub with water and turn off the faucet before putting your cat in the tub. A running faucet or hose only serves to terrify your cat, so try your best to avoid using these during the bath. Use the existing water in the tub, which should come up no higher than the elbows, to wet the hair for the shampoo. Plan ahead of time and have containers filled with clean water ready for the rinse that follows. Rinse a few times, drain the tub of the dirty bath water, then rinse some more. If you have to use the faucet while your cat is in the tub, turn it on only briefly. You'll find that this does wonders for your pet's (and your) nerves.

Most cats feel more comfortable if they have something to hold on to when getting bathed. Place an old window screen or air conditioner fil-

Even though cats self-groom, there will come a time when a bath is needed. When grooming is introduced during kittenhood, all the procedures (even bathing) become easier.

ter in the tub to provide a surface to cling to. Oftentimes, cats will hold firm to this, not budging a muscle, throughout the entire bath.

Try bathing in a different location each time. Cats tend to associate locations with bad (or good) experiences. Consequently, if bath time was a bit stressful last time, you may find that the mere sight of the same tub and location turns the bathing process into a rodeo the next time. Sometimes simply using another tub or sink rather than the one you used last time can defuse a potentially volatile situation.

Sometimes a cat simply refuses to take a bath regardless of what special steps you've taken. In this case, sedation may be required. If so, let your veterinarian perform the bath to ensure the safety and well-being of both you and your pet. Never let anyone but a licensed veterinarian administer a sedative or tranquilizer to your pet. If you do, it could be disastrous.

Dry Baths

Although not nearly as effective as wet baths, dry baths are indicated in those instances when a pet is ill or recovering from an illness and you wish to keep stress to a minimum. Dry baths are also useful for puppies and kittens less than eight weeks of age, and for pregnant dogs and cats. Cornstarch and baby powder both have been used with varying degrees of effectiveness, yet with the same degree of messiness. Your best bet is to purchase one of the many commercial dry shampoos and mousses available for this purpose from your pet health care professional.

Tips for Removing Foreign Matter and Odors

If you encounter tar, paint, gum, or other foreign matter stuck to the hair, there is no need to despair. Most of these substances can be cosmetically trimmed off with scissors or clippers in a matter of seconds. If this cannot be done without dire consequences for the coat's appearance, or if the substance is near the skin, the following guidelines should aid in removal.

Burrs: Moisten and soften the affected area with mineral oil, then comb out.

Tar/Paint: The most efficient way to remove these items is to wait for them to harden, then simply cut them off.

Oil and Grease: Apply plain soap or spot-treat with a waterless mechanic's hand cleaner to dissolve the grease and oil. Shampoo and rinse thoroughly. Repeat as needed.

Gum: Apply a piece of ice to the gum to first harden it, then remove it with scissors, forceps, or your fingers.

Skunk Odor: For pets that have come face to face with a skunk, bathing with soap and water, followed by a rinse consisting of a dilute chlorophyll solution or diluted household ammonia (4 teaspoons per gallon [20 mL per 4 L] of water) should

Owners who use good grooming techniques often find their pets' overall health and well-being is significantly enhanced.

help remove most of the smell. Products especially designed for removing skunk odor are also available from veterinarians and pet shops. Don't get discouraged: three or more treatments may be needed before the odor is eliminated completely.

Anal Sac Odor: Isopropyl alcohol followed by soap and water will usually rid the coat of the secretions and odor. Scented baby wipes can also be quite effective for removing this type of odor.

Chapter Five

Advanced Cosmetic Grooming Techniques

This chapter will be of special interest to those pet owners interested in cosmetically grooming their pets. Clipping and scissoring techniques are described, with emphasis on those cuts most commonly performed by professional groomers. The clips covered here are designed for pets, not show dogs. In addition, these cosmetic grooming techniques are useful for sprucing up an already existing haircut or style, but are not a substitute for periodic professional grooming. Following the patterns and lines established by a professional groomer is much easier (and much more aesthetically pleasing) than trying to establish these yourself on your pet's coat. Don't be afraid to ask your groomer if you can watch as your pet is being groomed. Not only will this give you a chance to have your questions answered, but you will also be able to see firsthand the proper way to hold and use grooming instruments. For further information on cosmetic grooming and on particular clips not covered here, consult one of the grooming books that professional groomers

use. Most of these are available at your favorite bookstore or local library. Before you can achieve the desired results from at-home cosmetic grooming, you will need to invest in some additional equipment and acquire some special skills above and beyond those needed for basic home grooming purposes. A good set of clippers (such as Oster Model A5) and a variety of clipper blades are a must; thinning shears and a pair of curved scissors would also be helpful. You will need to learn the fundamentals of cosmetic clipping and familiarize yourself with the terms *scissoring, thinning, plucking,* and *stripping.* This is the focus of this chapter. In the next chapter cosmetic grooming techniques for some of the more popular breeds of dogs is presented.

Clipping

To an uninitiated pet, the sound of a set of clippers can be quite unnerving. To help alleviate the tension, turn the clippers on and allow

When working around the face with scissors, always keep them parallel to the eyes.

your pet to become accustomed to the noise before actually employing them. Hold the apparatus as you would a pencil, balancing it so that its weight is evenly distributed on both sides. This will allow you to maneuver the clippers with more agility. Keep in mind that the higher the blade number, the closer the cut.

When using them, keep the blades parallel to the surface you are cutting. Follow the lie of the hair as if it were a roadmap, using smooth, gentle strokes. Whenever you note the hair growth changing direction, compensate with a semicircular stroke. Never force the blade through the hair faster than it can cut it. This not only will damage the blade but will also lead to clipper burns (see "Clipper Burns," page 108). Let the clipper set the pace as it cuts. Finally, always have a

can of clipper lubricant spray on hand. This should be sprayed directly onto the blades during a clipping procedure whenever the blades become warm to prevent an inadvertent burning of the skin. The spray will also keep the blades well lubricated and help maintain their cutting efficiency. Products such as clipper lubricant can be purchased at most stores that carry grooming products. For added protection, also consider purchasing a clipper disinfectant spray to prevent the spread of disease during and after clipper use (see the discussion of clipper care on page 24).

Scissoring

The term *scissoring* applies to the use of scissors to "round off" rough

When clipping, use care around sensitive structures.

Thinning the coat of an Irish Wolfhound.

edges of the hair coat after clipping and to remove hair from those places inaccessible or inappropriate for clippers. Scissoring is undoubtedly the hardest part of cosmetic grooming. It requires patience and practice. Control is important, not only from the standpoint of results, but also in terms of safety. To help achieve this control, be sure to grip the scissors properly. Place your thumb in the large hole of the scissors, and your ring finger (not your middle finger) in the smaller hole. Then, rest your little finger on the scissors' finger rest (if present). This hand placement will afford you the mobility to do the job correctly. When scissoring, always use a smooth, steady motion and avoid "thrusting" the scissors at the hair. When working around the eyes, keep the blades parallel to the eyelids to avoid injury should your pet fidget.

Before scissoring can begin, your pet must be willing to stay completely calm and still during the procedure. If this is not the case, the use of the scissors should be abandoned. Otherwise, the danger of injury is too great. (See "A Word About Safety," page 17.)

Thinning

Thinning is a procedure that employs thinning shears to blend different portions of the coat together and remove excess telogen (shed) hairs from the coat (see "The Hair

Coat," page 80). When using thinning shears, always thin with the grain or lie of the hair, never against, for if it is done against the grain, more hairs may be pulled out than desired, leaving patchy "holes" in the coat.

Plucking and Stripping

These two procedures are usually limited to terriers and other wiry-coated breeds being groomed for show. Both involve the manual removal of the actual hair from its follicle while it is in telogen, or the shedding phase of the hair cycle. By removing this dead hair prematurely, a new, fresh coat can be achieved more quickly. It is also said that a truer, richer hair color and the desired rough texture of the coat are achieved by employing this technique.

Stripping uses a tool called a *stripping comb* to remove the hair, whereas plucking is done with the fingers. Because it is often difficult to differentiate those hairs in the telogen stage from those in other stages, plucking or stripping can be quite uncomfortable for the pet. As a result, many groomers opt to use the brush and clippers in place of these techniques. Proper restraint is warranted if your pet is not accustomed to the plucking or stripping process.

When plucking, use the thumb and forefinger to grasp a small amount of hair. Pull downward sharply and quickly to remove the telogen hairs.

This excess hair between the toes of a Welsh Corgi needs to go!

Repeat this process over those desired portions of the coat.

If using a stripping comb, grasp the tool with four fingers, then use the thumb to press a small patch of hair against the blade. Jerk the blade in the direction of the hair growth, effectively removing the patch of hair. Continue, doing small portions at a time.

Choosing a Groomer

At one time or another, you may decide to use the services of a professional groomer. With so many to choose from, selecting the right groomer can be difficult. There are, however, ways to narrow the choices.

Probably the most reliable way to find a good groomer is by word of mouth. Ask your friends and neighbors whom they use. If the same name keeps popping up, that is probably the one to try. If you fail to get any leads this way, consult the phone book and newspaper, or visit a local dog show. Consider choosing a groomer that is close to (or in some cases, part of) your veterinarian's office or local boarding kennel just in case a problem arises during the grooming session.

Regardless of how you locate your groomer, take the time to actually talk to him or her in person before making a final decision. Does this groomer seem genuinely caring toward animals? Are the facilities clean? Does the groomer have pictures or a portfolio of his or her work? What is the protocol in case of a grooming injury or an emergency?

There are various organizations that set standards of quality and guidelines for the grooming profession as a whole. One is the International Professional Groomers, Inc. (IPG). Professional groomers certified by the IPG can be found throughout the United States and other countries, including Canada and England. Grooming skills and expertise, as well as ethical behavior, are just a few of the criteria that govern certification by this group.

Other groups, such as the National Dog Groomers Association of America, publish similar guidelines designed to assure quality within the industry. For information pertaining to certified pet groomers in your area, contact one of the organizations listed on page 111.

Once you've finally decided, take your pet to meet the new groomer. Don't just drop your pet off and leave; be sure to hang around for the first few minutes of interaction between the groomer and your pet. This will make your four-legged friend feel more at ease.

Before you depart, be sure to leave a number where you can be reached and the number and name of your veterinarian. That way, if your pet becomes overly upset or if an accident happens, both you and your veterinarian can be contacted right away. Note: Beware of the groomer who tries to diagnose and/or treat ailments or injuries without consulting a veterinarian. Not only is this unethical and illegal behavior, but it is also endangering your pet's health. The same is true for tranquilization. This is to be performed only by a licensed veterinarian.

Chapter Six

Cosmetic Grooming of Select Breeds

Cocker Spaniels

The cosmetic grooming procedures in this section apply only to pet Cocker Spaniels. Show dogs are groomed differently.

Recommended equipment: a brush and comb, Oster A5 clippers with a #10 and #7F blade, scissors, and thinning shears. Cosmetic grooming should be performed on your Cocker Spaniel every three to five weeks. Before starting, brush your dog thoroughly to remove any mats and tangles (see "Removing Mats and Tangles," page 43). Then bathe and fluff-dry.

Head: Using the #10 blade, clip from just behind the eyebrow region back to the base of the skull. Leave a small "dome" above the eyebrows. Clip the muzzle, cheeks, and lower jaw, directing your motion against the grain of the hair. Clip the throat area in a V shape, from the angles of the lower jaw to the top of the sternum.

Ears: Using a #10 blade, clip the top third of the ear both inside and out. Carefully scissor the outside edges of the clipped portion of the ear until all fuzzy hairs are removed.

Abdomen: Holding your dog up on its hind legs, clip the belly region from the navel to a point just in front of the genital area using a #10 blade. Be careful to avoid cutting the folds of skin in the dog's flanks.

Body: Using a #7F blade, clip from the base of the skull and proceed down the back until you reach the base of the tail. Always follow the grain or lie of the hair. Then, starting at the shoulders, proceed again back toward the tail, but this time use a downward motion with your clippers on each side of the body to effectively "blend" the cut portion with the rest of the long coat.

The Cocker Spaniel.

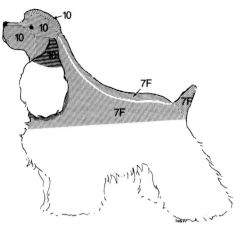

Blade selection (side view).

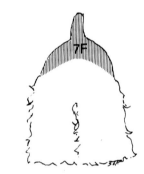

Blade selection (rear view).

Blade selection (front view).

Perform this blending all the way to the base of the tail.

Tail: This area is clipped using a #7F blade. Start at the base of the tail and trim toward the end, following the lie of the hair.

Blending: Using the thinning shears, thin the hair at the clipped-unclipped junction of the coat. This blending of the two lengths of the hair will make the pattern you just performed look more natural.

Feet: Scissor between the pads of the four paws, removing all excess hair. Then, scissor around the perimeter of the feet, making the cut edges of the hair even with the table surface.

Schnauzers

Recommended equipment: a brush and comb, Oster A5 clippers with #10 and #9 blades, scissors, and thinning shears. Cosmetic grooming should be performed on your Schnauzer every four to six weeks. Before starting, brush your dog thoroughly to remove any mats and tangles (see "Removing Mats and Tangles," page 43). Then bathe and fluff-dry.

Clipping

Head: Using the eyebrows and the corners of the mouth as markers, use a #10 blade to clip the head and lower jaw, starting from a point just behind your markers and extending to just behind the base of the ears. When clipping, use parallel horizontal strokes, following the lie of the hair. Do not clip any of the hair on the muzzle.

Ears: A #10 blade is used for the ears. Because the ear flaps are too soft to stand up against the weight of the clippers, each one must be supported firmly with your free hand. Follow the grain of the hair out from the center of the ear to the edges.

Abdomen: Lifting your dog by its front legs (with its hind legs still touching the table), clip the belly region from the navel to a point just in front of the genital area using a #10 blade. Be careful to avoid cutting the folds of skin in the dog's flanks.

Body: Using a #9 blade, clip from the base of the skull and proceed down the back until you reach the base of the tail. Always follow the grain or lie of the hair. Continue clipping the body down to an imaginary parallel line running from a point just above the elbows on the front legs and extending back through the top portions of the flank folds and on back to the hind end. The hind legs are then clipped on a diagonal line from the folds of the flank to a point just above the hocks, leaving fringes of hair on the front third of the legs. The front legs are left unclipped. Finally, the front portion of the neck and chest are clipped starting at the neck-head junction and ending at the sternum.

Tail: Using a #9 blade, clip the top, sides, and bottom of the tail, trimming to a slight taper at the end. Use caution to avoid the anus when clipping beneath the tail.

The Schnauzer.

Once the clipping is complete, the final touch is applied by careful scissoring.

Scissoring

Feet: Scissor between the pads of all four paws, removing all excess hair. Then, scissor around the perimeter of the feet, making the cut edges of the hair even with the table surface. The toenails should not be exposed.

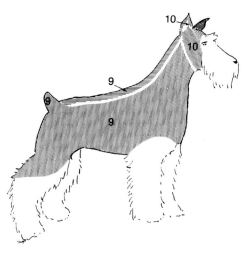

Blade selection (side view).

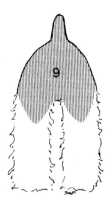

Blade selection (rear view).

Blade selection (front view).

Legs: Holding the scissors with the ends facing upward, trim the legs in a circular fashion, making them cylindrical in appearance. The back legs should be scissored in a similar fashion. Use your scissors or thinning shears to blend the hair at the junctions between the clipped and the unclipped portions of the hair coat.

Chest: Scissor the hair in this region from the point of the sternum to the flank region.

Eyebrows: Schnauzers have long, parted eyebrows, so begin by scissoring the hair between the eyes. Combing the eyebrows forward, scissor the eyebrow hair into an inverted V shape. Start at the highest point of the eyebrows and trim at a 45-degree angle in the direction of the top corner of the ear on the opposite side of the head.

Ears: Scissor the outside edges slowly and carefully until the fuzzy hairs are removed.

Muzzle: Comb the hair on the muzzle forward. Then, using your scissors and thinning shears, remove any uneven or excessively long hairs.

Poodles

As you may know, there are many ways to clip a Poodle. Described below is the Kennel Clip, one of the most popular and easy clips for pet Poodles. Ideally, cosmetic grooming should be performed on Poodles every three to five weeks.

Recommended equipment: a brush and comb, Oster A5 clippers with #10, #15, and #4F blades, and scissors. Before starting, brush thoroughly to remove any mats and tangles (see "Removing Mats and Tangles," page 43). Then bathe and fluff-dry.

Preliminary Procedures

A number of preliminary procedures must be carried out regardless of the type of clip you maintain on your Poodle.

Feet: The poodle is the only breed of dog that has its feet shaved. A #15 blade can be used to accomplish this task. Clip the front and sides of the foot, starting from the toenails and proceeding back behind the large pad of the foot. Now clip between the toes and pads using a side-to-side motion, being careful not to cut any skin webbing.

Head and Face: Use a #10 blade when clipping the face on light-colored dogs, and a #15 on dark-colored dogs. Keep the clipper flat against the skin surface to avoid clipper abrasions. Clip from the corner of the eye to the ear on both sides of the head, following a horizontal line. This first clip sets the boundaries for the topknot. Aiming the clippers at a 45-degree angle, clip the muzzle from the inside corners of the eyes to the end of the nose. Clip the bridge of the nose, starting near the eyes and working toward the end. Holding the dog's muzzle up in the air, clip from where the neck and head meet to the end of the lower jaw.

Mustaches: Many Poodle owners like to have a mustache on their pet's muzzle. If desired, simply omit clipping the hair on the muzzle anywhere from a point starting at the corners of the mouth and extending forward to the tip of the nose. Shape the mustache in any form or fashion you desire by using scissors.

Tail: The tail of the Poodle can vary in appearance, depending on owner preference, so there is really no set way to clip it. To achieve the pom-pom look, clip the hair off the front third of the tail only. Keep the blade flat, and avoid the anal region.

The Poodle.

Topknot, Tail, and Ears: Scissor all of these areas to achieve a rounded effect. The first cut should be made in a straight line parallel to the top of the head. Then continue trimming around the head, being careful not to cut the hair too flat or too short for your taste. The tail is done in essentially the same manner, trying to create a rounded appearance. Comb out the hair on

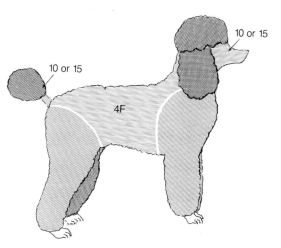

Blade selection (side view).

the ears and scissor off any excessively long, uneven hairs.

Abdomen: Lifting your dog by its front legs (with its hind legs still touching the table), clip the belly region from the navel to a point just in front of the genital area using a #10 blade. Be careful to avoid cutting the folds of skin in the dog's flanks.

Kennel Clip

Body: Use a #4F blade for this clip. Start at the base of the neck and clip straight down the back toward the tail. Be sure to stay above the level of the shoulders and hips when doing this. Next, avoiding the hair on the legs from the shoulders and hips on down toward the feet, clip the entire body between the elbows and folds of the flank, following the grain of the hair. After clipping, brush the clipped hair upward against the grain and scissor any uneven hair. Do the same for the unclipped hair on the legs to achieve a rounded appearance. Neatly trim the base of the legs where the hair meets the shaved feet.

The Scottish Terrier.

Scottish Terriers

Recommended equipment: a brush and comb, Oster A5 clippers with #10 and #7F blades, scissors, and thinning shears. Cosmetic grooming should be performed on your Scottie every four to six weeks. Before starting, brush thoroughly to remove mats and tangles (see "Removing Mats and Tangles" page 43). Then bathe and towel- or fluff-dry.

Clipping

Head: Using the eyebrows and the corners of the mouth as markers, use a #10 blade to clip the head and lower jaw, starting from a point just behind your markers and extending to just behind the base of the ears. Do not clip any of the hair on the muzzle. When clipping, use parallel horizontal strokes, following the lie of the hair.

Ears: A #10 blade is also used for the ears. Only the top half of the ear is to be clipped, leaving a tuft of hair at the base and front inside edge of each ear. Follow the grain of the hair from the center of the ear to the edges.

Abdomen: Lifting your dog by its front legs (with its hind legs still touching the table), clip the belly region from the navel to a point just in front of the genital area using a #10 blade. Be careful to avoid cutting the folds of skin in the dog's flanks.

Body: Using a #7F blade, start at the base of the skull and proceed down the back until you reach the base of the tail. Always follow the grain or lie of the hair. Continue clipping the body surface down to an imaginary parallel line running from the front point of the sternum back to the genital region. Everything below this line will remain unclipped. Finally, the front portion of the neck and chest are clipped starting at the neck-head junction and ending at the top of the sternum.

Tail: Using a #7F blade, clip the entire top portion of the tail.

Blade selection (side view).

Scissoring

Feet: Scissor between the pads of the four paws, removing all excess hair. Then, scissor around the perimeter of the feet, making the cut edges of the hair even with the table surface. The toenails should not be exposed.

Legs: Holding the scissors with the ends facing upward, trim the legs in a circular fashion, making them cylindrical in appearance. Scissor the back legs in a similar fashion.

Body: Scissor the hair on the unclipped portion of the body. Next, use scissors or thinning shears to blend the hair at the junctions between the clipped and the unclipped portions of the hair coat.

Chest: Scissor the hair in this region from the point of the sternum to the flank.

Eyebrows: Scotties have long, parted eyebrows, so begin by scissoring the hair between the eyes. Combing the eyebrows forward, scissor the eyebrow hair into an inverted V shape. Start at the high-

est point of the eyebrows and trim at a 45-degree angle in the direction of the top corner of the ear on the opposite side of the head. The hair

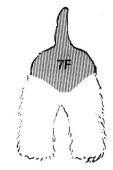

Blade selection (rear view).

Blade selection (front view).

on the inner portion of the brow should remain longer than that on the outer portion.

Ears: Scissor the outside edges slowly and carefully until all fuzzy hairs are removed.

Muzzle: Comb the hair on the muzzle forward. Then, using your scissors and thinning shears, remove any uneven or excessively long hairs. Shape as desired.

Wire Fox and Welsh Terriers

Recommended equipment: a brush and comb, Oster A5 clippers with #10 and #8½ blades, scissors, and thinning shears. Cosmetic grooming should be performed on these terriers every four to six weeks.

Before starting, brush thoroughly to remove any mats and tangles (see "Removing Mats and Tangles," page 43). Then bathe and towel- or fluff-dry. Plucking or stripping is optional.

The Welsh Terrier.

Clipping

Head: Using the eyebrows and the corners of the mouth as markers, use a #8½ blade to clip the head and lower jaw, starting from a point just behind your markers and extending to just behind the base of the ears. Do not clip any of the hair on the muzzle. When clipping, use parallel horizontal strokes, following the lie of the hair.

Ears: Using a #8½ blade, clip the entire outer surfaces of the ears. Follow the grain of the hair from the base of the ear to the edges.

Abdomen: Holding your dog up on its hind legs, clip the belly region from the navel to a point just in front of the genital area using a #10 blade. Be careful to avoid cutting the folds of skin in the dog's flanks.

Body: Using a #8½ blade, start at the base of the skull and proceed down the back until you reach the base of the tail. Always follow the grain or lie of the hair. Continue clipping the body down to an imaginary parallel line running from a point just above the elbows on the front legs through the top portions of the flank folds and on back to the hind end. The hind legs and front legs are left unclipped. Finally, the front portion of the neck and chest are clipped, starting at the neck-head junction and ending at the top of the sternum.

Tail: Using a #8½ blade, clip the top, sides, and bottom of the tail, trimming to a slight taper at the end. Use caution to avoid the anus when clipping beneath the tail.

Scissoring

Feet: Scissor between the pads of the four paws, removing all excess hair. Then, scissor around the perimeter of the feet, making the cut edges of the hair even with the table surface. The toenails should not be exposed.

Legs: Holding the scissors with the ends facing upward, trim the legs in a circular fashion, making them cylindrical in appearance. The back legs should be scissored in a similar fashion. Next, use scissors or thinning shears to blend the hair at the junctions between the clipped and the unclipped portions of the hair coat.

Chest: Scissor the hair in this region from the point of the sternum to the flank.

Eyebrows: These particular terriers have short, parted eyebrows. Begin by scissoring the hair between the eyes. Combing the eyebrows forward, scissor the eyebrow hair into an inverted V shape. Start at the highest point of the eyebrows and trim at a 45-degree angle in the direction of the top corner of the ear on the opposite side of the head. The hair on the inner portion of the brow should remain slightly longer than that on the outer portion.

Ears: Scissor the outside edges slowly and carefully until all fuzzy hairs are removed.

Muzzle: Comb the hair on the muzzle forward. Then, using your scissors and thinning shears, remove any uneven or excessively long hairs. Shape as desired.

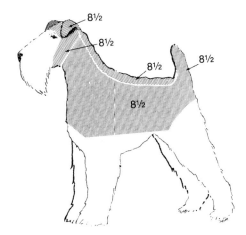

Blade selection (side view).

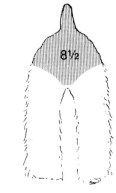

Blade selection (rear view).

Blade selection (front view).

Selected Parted-Coat Breeds

The Shih Tzu, Yorkshire Terrier, Maltese, and Lhasa Apso all have one thing in common: they all have long coats parted down the middle. Their body styles are all groomed alike, but the heads differ for each breed. The Shih Tzu, Yorkshire Terrier, and Maltese all have topknots tied in bows. The Shih Tzu and Yorkie use one bow; the Maltese uses two. All four of these breeds should be groomed every two to three weeks to keep their hair coats in excellent condition.

Recommended equipment: a pin brush or natural bristle brush, soft slicker brush, comb, scissors, Oster A5 clipper with a #10 blade, bows, and small rubber bands. If a short clip is desired on these breeds, a #4 blade should be used for this purpose.

The Shih Tzu.

Brush-Out: The brush-out is the most important part of grooming a parted breed. Long, fine, silky coats should always be moistened with water or conditioner during brushing to prevent the buildup of static electricity, which can damage the hair. Do not saturate the coat; just spray on a fine mist. Start brushing the feet using a pin brush, or a soft slicker brush if the dog is matted. Lifting the outer coat, mist the hair with conditioner and brush from the skin outward, a few hairs at a time. Use a comb only to check for tangles. Layer-brush the entire coat in this manner. Then bathe and fluff-dry the dog.

Finishing: Use scissors to trim excess hair from around and between the footpads. Then, if necessary, round off the outside edges of the feet, using the table as your guide. Using your comb, part the hair down the center of the back, starting at the top of the head and moving toward the base of the tail. Once finished, comb the hair straight down on both sides.

Shih Tzu

Topknot: To form the Shih Tzu topknot, part the hair from the outside corner of the eye to the corner of the ear. Grasp the hair evenly with one hand and with the other wrap a rubber band around the topknot. Place a bow at the base of the topknot.

Yorkshire Terriers

Ears: Clip the top third of the ears and scissor the outside edges smooth.

The Yorkshire Terrier.

The Maltese.

Topknot: With the hair already parted down the center of the head, part the hair again from the outside corner of the eye to the inside top corner of the ear. Then, part the hair across the head from ear to ear. Grasp the hair evenly with one hand and with the other wrap a small rubber band around the topknot. Place a bow at the base of the topknot.

Maltese

Topknot: The Maltese topknot is tied with two bows. Gather the hair by parting from the corner of the eye back to the inside corner of the ear on either side, and then across the top of the head from ear to ear. Grasp the topknot and use a comb to divide it into two portions. Each portion or side should then be doubled over and secured with a rubber band.

Lhasa Apsos

Topknot: Lhasas are usually shown without a topknot, with their hair parted down the middle the nat-

ural way. However, if a pet owner so chooses, a topknot similar to those used for the other parted-coat breeds can be used.

Mixed Breeds

All the various styles of clips and cuts can be used on mixed breeds, depending upon what appeals to the owners. If you know the genetic

The Lhasa Apso.

Clipper Blades for Dog Grooming

Clipper Blade Size	Blade Set Cut Length (cutting against the grain of the hair)*	Comments
4F	3/8" (9.5 mm)	Excellent for body work on Poodles. Creates smooth, velvety finish similar to that achieved by hand-scissoring. It is also the blade of choice for short clips on the small, parted-coated breeds.
7F	1/8" (3.2 mm)	Commonly used for back work on the Cocker Spaniel and Scottish Terrier breeds. Gives a smooth, textured look to the coat.
8 1/2	5/64" (2.0 mm)	An all-purpose blade that is ideal for terriers. Can also be used for the body work on Schnauzers if a longer finish is desired.
9	1/16" (1.6 mm)	This blade gives a medium cut and a smooth finish. It leaves a textured, natural look on the body of a Schnauzer.
10	1/16" (1.6 mm)	All-purpose blade commonly used for head work on Cocker Spaniels, Poodles, Schnauzers, and terriers. Can also be used for body work on Schnauzers.
15	3/64" (1.2 mm)	A good, all-purpose Poodle blade. Often used for trimming the feet, face, and tail of Poodles.
40	1/125" (0.1 mm)	Provides surgical-grade clip to the regions to which it is applied. Can also be useful for removing mats close to the skin.

*When cutting with the grain of the hair, these lengths will approximately double.

recipe that went into making your particular pet, you may want to use the breed cuts of the parents. Coarse-haired dogs look the best in terrier-type clips. Poodle-type clips can also be used on a variety of mixed breeds, yet you may not want to shave the feet of these dogs because many have large feet. Good-looking short clips, which are easy to do and care for, can be best achieved using a #4F clipper blade. Be imaginative and create the style that best suits your dog. Regardless of which clip you choose, remember that you can always change it when the dog needs to be clipped again.

Chapter Seven

Disorders of the Skin and Hair Coat

Disorders of the skin and coat are the most prevalent types of ailments seen in pets by veterinarians across the country. Skin diseases can outnumber other medical disorders by as much as three to one, especially in areas with hot climates. If you own a pet that has never experienced such a problem, consider yourself fortunate! *Dermatopathies,* the technical name for all disorders of the skin, come in many shapes and sizes, from simple flea-bite dermatitis to complex metabolic and immune system diseases. In fact, there can be more than 50 different causes of hair loss alone in dogs and cats. Unfortunately, because each complaint can have a wide range of potential causes, diagnosing exactly what is going on can be difficult. Determining whether the problem is primary (occurring by itself) or secondary (occurring because of some other underlying disease condition) can be challenging as well. To give you some insight, let's see how a dermatopathy dilemma is approached from a veterinary perspective.

Diagnosis

The first factor to be considered when trying to determine the cause of a dermatopathy is its history of occurrence. Does the problem come and go with the seasons? If so, it could suggest allergies. Are any other pets (or people) in the family suffering from a similar skin disorder? If the answer is "yes," the cause could be something that is contagious to other pets and possibly to people, such as fleas, mange, or ringworm. Is the dog or cat exhibiting other symptoms of disease not seemingly related to the skin problem, such as increased water consumption, increased urination, lethargy, or weight gain? If so, the skin problem may signal some type of metabolic disturbance, such as diabetes, affecting your pet's health. A recent change in diet may indicate a food allergy. Have any new medications been given recently? Allergies to medications, called *drug eruptions,* can occur, and must be ruled out as a potential cause of the dermatopathy. Finally, have any changes been made in the household or the normal daily routine that may have precipitated the onset of the dermatopathy? Stress-related loss of hair has been known to occur in both dogs and cats in response to sudden changes in routine.

Once a thorough history has been obtained and evaluated, attention should be focused on the type of pet involved. First, consider age. Although all age groups can be affected, dermatopathies can be more prevalent in one age class than another. For instance, when a pet of less than one year of age is involved, parasitic, congenital (present at birth), and nutritional causes of dermatopathies should come to mind. Also, although allergies may affect pets of all ages, they appear much more frequently in the young to middle-aged adult dog and cat. If the pet in question happens to be older, cancer-related skin disease or metabolic disturbances such as a thyroid disorder should be considered.

Next, what breed of pet is involved? Certain breeds of dogs and cats are more predisposed to specific skin and hair coat disorders than others. For example, self-inflicted dermatitis and hair loss caused by nervous licking or chewing seems to be more common in Siamese and Abyssinian cats than in other breeds. The incidence of hypothyroidism seems to be higher in Doberman Pinschers and Cocker Spaniels than in Poodles. In turn, Beagles, Schnauzers, Poodles, and terriers have a higher incidence of allergies than do other canine breeds.

A close look at the distribution of the skin disease or hair loss provides further clues as to the origin of a skin problem. For instance, flea allergy dermatitis in dogs almost always presents as hair loss with or without secondary skin infection along the back near the tail and along the hind legs. The symmetry of the lesions is also important. Lesions and hair loss that are symmetrical in appearance (that is, affecting similar locations on both the right and left side of the body) indicate that some type of generalized disturbance is going on, such as a metabolic disease or an allergy. In contrast, lesions that do not exhibit symmetry can often be attributed to parasites, skin infections, or other localized causes.

The primary symptoms associated with a dermatopathy will help narrow the potential causes even more. Certainly of all the complaints about the skin and coat of dogs and cats, itching and hair loss top the list. No pet owner would deny that it is frustrating to have an itchy pet. The relentless scratching and chewing, with enough tufts of torn-out hair lying around to knit a sweater, not only drive your pet crazy, but can drive you insane as well. Anything that can cause skin inflammation can cause itching. In dogs and cats, the two most notable culprits are skin parasites and allergies. However, don't be too hasty to set the blame on these. Other disorders can cause similar signs as well.

Clinical Signs Related to Various Skin Conditions

Itching with hair loss	Skin parasites, allergies, skin infections, seborrhea, nutritional deficiency
Itching without hair loss	Same as above, yet in early stages, also ear infection if scratching at head
Hair loss without itching	Hormonal imbalances, ringworm, telogen defluxion, demodectic mange, nutritional deficiency, neuro-dermatitis
Dry, flaky skin	Seborrhea sicca, bacterial skin infection, nutritional deficiency, excessive bathing, lack of brushing
Oily, greasy skin and hair	Seborrhea oleosa, *Malazzia* dermatitis, stud tail (cats), lack of grooming (especially in sick cats)
Scabby, crusty skin	Skin infection, mange, allergies, seborrhea, feline military dermatitis
Bad odor to skin and hair coat	Seborrhea, skin infection, ear infection, periodontal disease, anal sacs
Thickened skin with hair loss	Skin callus, hypothyroidism, any chronic (long-term) skin disease
Color (pigment) changes to the skin and/or hair	Genetic abnormality, trauma to the skin (physical or chemical), any chronic (long-term) skin disease, acanthosis nigricans, skin cancer, hormone-related dermatopathies
Small red bumps and/or pustules on skin surface	Atopy, allergic reaction, skin infection/folliculitis, parasites (such as mange mites)
Lumps and masses	Abscess, lipoma, skin tumor, granuloma, cyst
Raw, moist, open sores on skin	Hot spot, lick granuloma, eosinophilic granuloma (cats), solar dermatitis, skin tumor, feline military dermatitis
Excessive grooming/licking	Neurodermatitis/behavioral, lick granuloma, skin parasites, skin infection, trauma (physical/chemical); urinary tract infection (excessive grooming in genital region)

Hair loss is often the unhappy by-product of the pet's relentless chewing and scratching, and of the inflammation affecting the hair follicles. Because itching and loss of hair tend to go hand in hand, it is difficult to talk about one without the other. However, realize that both do not always have to occur together. As we will see later, one hallmark of metabolic skin disease in pets is hair loss without any accompanying itching or scratching. Similarly, the fungal infection known as ringworm may appear as hair loss without any noticeable scratching, assuming the inflammation caused by the organism is minimal. Is it possible to see itching without loss of hair? It is, especially in the early stages of any skin disease. However, if relief from the itching and inflammation is not swift, hair will soon start to fall out.

Besides itching and hair loss, dermatopathies can assume a number of different presentations. Some of the more common signs and appearances observed in dog and cat skin diseases, as well as the potential causes for each, are listed in the table on page 73.

As we have just seen, many factors need to be taken into account when attempting to diagnose the cause of a dermatopathy in a pet. What appears to be a clear-cut case of fleas may actually turn out to be something completely different. This is where your veterinarian can help. Don't try to diagnose your pet's skin condition yourself! The guidelines presented here are meant to give you some idea of what might be occurring, but for a definitive diagnosis, expert attention is essential. The goal is not to obtain a diagnosis, but to obtain a correct diagnosis!

When you take your pet to your veterinarian for a skin evaluation, expect certain diagnostic tests to be performed. The table on page 76 lists some of these helpful diagnostic tests and the purposes for doing them. Many times a trained eye can make a diagnosis immediately; other times a whole series of tests is required to uncover the cause of the skin disease. It is in your pet's best interest to have them done.

Treating dermatopathies can be just as difficult and involved as diagnosing them. Any treatment performed should first be directed toward the underlying disease that may be causing the skin condition, then against the lesions involving the actual skin and coat. Traditionally, antibiotics, corticosteroids (anti-inflammatory medications), and insecticidal preparations, used alone or in combination, have been the standard treatment for almost all types of dermatopathies in dogs and cats. However, in recent years, new drugs, supplements, and medications (such as cyclosporine A) have been developed to complement these conventional therapies and, in many cases, replace them. This is certainly good news for those pets that are at risk from the potentially dangerous side effects of long-term corticosteroid use. As each of the following dermatopathies are examined more closely, the treatment alternatives are discussed further.

Skin Parasites

Fleas

Fleas, particularly the common cat flea (*Ctenocephalides felis*), are by far the most irritating pests encountered by dog and cat owners and their four-legged companions. With flea allergy dermatitis (see page 85) accounting for the majority of skin disease cases seen by veterinarians each year, millions of dollars are spent on flea-control products and services alone in a desperate attempt to provide relief to itchy dogs and cats. This control becomes even more important because of the fact that dogs and cats aren't the only ones fleas annoy. If they get hungry enough, fleas attack people as well! In this respect, they can become a direct public health threat, because fleas are known carriers of diseases such as endemic typhus and bubonic plague. Fleas can also suck enough blood to cause anemia in severely infested pets (especially kittens), and are the known intermediate host for the common dog and cat tapeworm. But the good news is that recent scientific advances have achieved tremendous victories in the war against fleas, and have greatly eased the burden on pet owners who, in past years, assumed such a conflict could never be won.

The life cycle of the flea requires two weeks to two years to complete, depending on environmental conditions. Maturity occurs most rapidly when the temperature is between 65°F (18°C) and 95°F (35°C) and the relative humidity is between 50 and 99 percent (no wonder they are such a problem in warm climates!).

After enjoying their first blood meal as adults, fleas rarely leave a pet, desiring instead to stick close to their source of food. Eventually, the

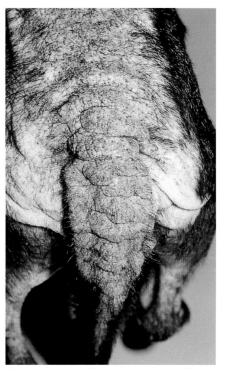

A severe case of flea allergy dermatitis.

female fleas start to lay 40 to 50 eggs per day, which then fall off the host and are deposited directly into the environment where the pet plays, eats, or sleeps. The white wormlike larvae that emerge from the eggs prefer to avoid light and spend their time feeding on adult flea excrement ("flea dirt"), which is nothing more than digested blood, or other particles of organic material found in the environment. When the larvae mature 9 to 200 days later, they spin a cocoon and become pupae. Pupae remain encased within their shells for seven days to a year, depending upon environmental conditions. Once

Diagnostic Aids for Dermatopathies

Test	Purpose
Skin scraping	Detects mange mites, other parasites
DTM (Dermatophyte Test Medium)	Tests for the presence of ringworm
Woods Lamp (ultraviolet light)	Tests for the presence of ringworm
Cytology	Miscroscopic examination of fluid or cells from skin lesions; preliminary test for cancer
Skin biopsy	Microscopic examination of a tissue sample; definitive test for cancer and autoimmune diseases
Bacterial culture/sensitivity	Identifies types of bacteria involved in a skin infeciton; determines which antibiotics that particular organism is sensitive to
Blood and stool parasite checks	Detects internal parasites, some of which can cause itchy reactions
Complete blood count/serum biochemical profile	Identifies underlying internal diseases (such as diabetes, Cushing's disease, allergies, etc.)
Hormonal assay	Detects hormonally related dermatopathies
Allergy testing (skin testing or blood testing)	Helps determine what substances a pet is actually allergic to

they emerge, they immediately start looking for a host to feed on, using pressure changes, vibrations, or fluctuations in carbon dioxide levels to guide them to their first blood meal. And so the life cycle begins again.

Dogs infested with fleas will scratch, chew, and lose hair around the hind legs and the back, near the base of the tail. If you part the hair (or what's left of it) in these areas, you will often see the tiny black flecks of flea excrement that are left behind after feeding. In cats, fleas tend to hang out around the neck region rather than in the hindquarters. Because the scratching can be intense, it is common to find crusts and scabs lining the neck area of a cat infested with fleas (see "Miliary Dermatitis," page 105). As with dogs, look for the tiny black flecks—a sure sign that you and your cat are not alone!

Flea Control

The primary weapons in the pet owner's arsenal against fleas are the new generation insecticides and chemicals known as *insect growth regulators* (IGR) and *insect development inhibitors* (IDI). The new generation insecticides are highly effective at killing adult fleas, whereas IGRs and IDIs prevent flea eggs and larvae from maturing into adult fleas, thereby breaking the parasite's life cycle. See the table on pages 78–79 for a summary of the more popular ones available commercially.

But make no mistake about it: Even when using one of these newer products on your pet, flea control can still be challenging! For maximum control, regular treatment of the home and yard is still important. Your goal is to achieve complete, comprehensive, and ongoing control of fleas on your pet and in your environment. Fleas are notorious for their ability to develop resistance to insecticides. This occurs when only one type of treatment approach and chemical agent is employed in an inconsistent manner, killing off only the highly sensitive fleas in a population, leaving the hardier, more resistant ones to reproduce and pass on this resistance. As a result, be consistent and persistent in your flea control efforts, and use the following approach to minimize the development of flea resistance.

Treating Your Pet

For best results, ask your veterinarian which product listed in the table on page 78 you should use for your individual pet(s). He or she will be able to make an effective recommendation based on your pet's individual lifestyle. For example, if you have a dog that likes to swim, then imidacloprid, which washes off easily in water, would not be the best choice for your pet. In addition, products containing permethrin should never be used on cats. Finally, for puppies and kittens under eight weeks of age, a flea comb and a shampoo containing pyrethrins, natural and effective flea-killing substances derived from chrysanthemums, can be used to temporarily control fleas until the youngster is old enough for one of the newer products.

Apply these products as often as recommended by your veterinarian to ensure the highest level of efficacy. Beware of commercially available over-the-counter topical spot-ons or sprays that claim to be just as effective as those products listed in the table on page 78. Many of these contain strong agents that can be harmful to certain pets.

Treating Your House

Start your environment control program in your home by cleaning and vacuuming carpets, floors, and your pet's carrier and sleeping quarters, including all blankets and bedding, to remove dirt, eggs, and larvae. In addition to cleaning thoroughly beneath sofas, chairs, and other furniture, be sure to lift up and vacuum beneath seat cushions, pillows, and mattresses, giving extra attention to all cracks and crevices encountered. Vacuum bags should be disposed of afterward to get rid of any live fleas or flea larvae contained within. If your vacuum doesn't use a bag, consider adding mothballs to the machine's collection chambers to kill any larvae or fleas harvested.

Popular New Generation Flea Control Agents

Agent	Mode of Administration
Lufenuron (Program, Sentinel)	Oral, injectable
Selamectin (Revolution)	Topical spot-on*
S-methoprene	Oral, Topical
Pyriproxifen (Biospot; Knockout; Breakthru)	Topical spray, spot-on*, and collars
Imidacloprid (Advantage)	Topical spot-on*
Imidacloprid plus Permethrin (K9 Advantix)	Topical spot-on*
Fipronil (Frontline)	Topical spray and spot-on*
Nitenpyram (Capstar)	Oral

* Note: Topical spot-on products are applied as drops along the back of the neck and/or the back of the pet itself.

Next, set off a commercial insecticide fogger, preferably one containing an IGR, inside your house to kill adult fleas that you didn't get with vacuuming. (Be sure to remove all pets, including birds and fish, from the premises before doing so.) After the fogging is complete, sprinkle an orthoboric acid–based powder (available at your favorite pet supply store) to carpets and upholstery within the home. This product is deadly to flea larvae and will dry up newly laid eggs. The advantage of an orthoboric acid–based powder is that it works for up to a year after a single application, that is, unless you shampoo or steam clean your carpet or upholstery. In those instances, reapplication will be required.

Finally, six weeks after applying the orthoboric acid–based powder, fog once again. This is needed to kill any stray adults that may have emerged from the resistant pupal stage since the first fogger treatment.

Mode of Action	Comments
Inhibits development of flea eggs	High margin of safety; poorly absorbed unless given with fatty meal; Sentinel brand also contains medication to prevent canine heartworms
Kills adult fleas; prevents eggs from hatching	High margin of safety; can also be effective against sarcoptic mange and ticks; used to prevent canine heartworms
Insect growth regulator; kills eggs and larvae	Often combined with topical insecticides
Insect growth regulator	Often combined with synergized pyrethrins or permethrin; these combination products are not safe for cats
Kills adult fleas	High margin of safety; will wash off with swimming or bathing; can be reapplied often
Kills and repels adult fleas	Also repels mosquitoes; not for use on cats
Kills adult fleas	Safe for puppies and kittens 8 weeks and older; combined with s-methoprene in Frontline Plus; less likely to wash off than other topical products
Kills adult fleas	Rapid flea kill, yet very short acting (less than 24 hours)

Treating Your Yard

Most of the more common insecticides used to treat yards for fleas are available in granular form. When watered well into the lawn, they provide the best long-term flea control. Remember that flea larvae will seek out those regions of the yard providing shade, moisture, and elevated humidity (under decks, mobile homes, under shrubbery, and so on), so be sure to focus on these areas when treating. To help reduce the chances of a flea resistance forming against yard insecticides, vary the type (active ingredient) used whenever you retreat.

As an alternative to insecticides, *beneficial nematodes* can be used in the yard to control fleas. Beneficial nematodes are living organisms that feed on fleas. They are harmless to people and pets, and, when applied to a lawn, can be quite effective at ridding it of fleas. Their only drawback is that they tend to lose their

Ticks can carry diseases harmful to humans.

nated flea and tick collars are also useful for keeping these pests from attaching to your pet. If one does find its way through to your pet's skin, a topical flea and tick spray should be used to kill it. Most ticks will simply fall off in time once they have died; however, in some cases, you may need to manually remove them. When picking one off your pet, never use your bare hands. If you do and you happen to get any of the tick's bodily fluids on you, you could be exposing yourself to disease. Use tweezers or gloves instead. Grasp the tick as close to its head as possible and pull straight up, using constant tension. Once the tick has been removed, wash the bite wound with soap and water and then apply a first aid cream or ointment to prevent infection. Again, be sure the tick is completely dead before removal; this will ensure that the tick's mouthparts come out attached to the rest of the body. If left behind, the mouthparts can cause irritating localized reactions or bumps that can linger for quite some time.

effectiveness during the hot, dry months of summer when soil moisture is low. During these months, insecticide granules should be used instead of the nematodes.

Ticks

Like fleas, ticks pose a health risk not only to your pet, but to you as well. Ticks can cause damage to their host animal just by sheer numbers, causing loss of blood that may result in anemia. Their saliva can also be irritating and, in some cases, toxic. These parasites also transmit a number of diseases to both people and animals, including Rocky Mountain spotted fever, Lyme disease, and ehrlichiosis. For these reasons, controlling ticks is essential.

Fipronil (see the table on page 78) is highly effective at protecting your pet from ticks. Insecticide-impreg-

For controlling ticks in your pet's outdoor environment, use a yard and premise pesticide spray. Be sure to apply it not only to the lawn, but to the surrounding trees and shrubbery as well (make certain the pesticide is safe to use on your particular shrubbery before applying!).

And keep in mind that ticks can live for months in their surrounding habitat without a blood meal, so treat the environment every 3 to 4 weeks during the peak flea and tick seasons (April through October), and every 8 to 12 weeks during the remaining months.

Mites

Mange mites are likened to "microscopic ticks" that live within the skin or hair follicles and feed on body fluid, including blood and cellular debris. They often cause a crusty dermatitis that leads to hair loss and secondary infection. In all, there are four types of mange mites that are of special significance in dogs and cats.

Sarcoptic mange, caused by *Sarcoptes scabiei*, is characterized by itching, prominent hair loss, and/or thickened, wrinkled skin, especially around a dog's face, ear tips, elbows, thighs, and tail. Notoedric mange, caused by *Notoedres cati*, is the feline counterpart of the dog sarcoptic mange mite, and has a similar distribution pattern. Both of these mange mites actually burrow into the skin of their host; this induces inflammation and causes an intense itching sensation.

The mange mite, *Cheyletiella*—better known as "walking dandruff"—also causes a variable amount of itching in infested dogs and cats, but, unlike sarcoptic or notoedric mange, this mite lives primarily on the surface of the skin. It gets its name from the fact that if you look closely, the scales and dandruff produced by the infestation will appear to be moving or "walking" around, owing to the activity of the mite.

The demodectic mange mite, *Demodex canis*, resides within the hair follicles of its canine host, often causing secondary folliculitis and infection. By itself, it usually doesn't cause the severe itching we see with sarcoptic mange, but if the hair follicles become infected, itching can become a significant factor. Of all the mange mite infestations, Demodex is probably the most serious, especially in the older pet, because it usually indicates that some type of an immune disorder or immune suppression exists in the host animal. Because of this, it is often difficult to treat and cure in older pets. Cat owners don't have to worry as much about this type of mange, because

Demodectic mange on the face of a Chow Chow.

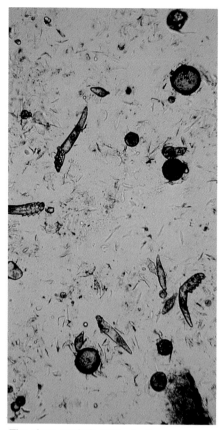

The characteristic "alligator" appearance of the Demodex mange mite.

demodectic mange (*Demodex cati*) is rare in the feline species. When it does occur, it is usually secondary to some type of immune suppression, such as that seen with feline leukemia or feline immunodeficiency viruses.

Your veterinarian will observe clinical signs and obtain and examine skin scrapings to diagnose mange in your dog or cat. It is essential that a proper diagnosis be made because treatments vary between the different types of mange. Two drugs,

ivermectin and selamectin, are commonly used by veterinarians to effectively treat most cases of mange in dogs. For select patients, a special insecticidal dip may be substituted. Regardless of the agent used, if a secondary skin infection is present, antibiotic therapy may be necessary as well.

Sarcoptes, Notoedres, and *Cheyletiella* are all contagious to humans, although the infestation is usually self-limiting. However, if your pet is diagnosed with one of these types of mange, and you or someone in your family has itchy skin lesions, be sure to contact your physician immediately.

Otodectes cynotis, better known as the ear mite, lives not in the skin or hair follicles, but in the external ear canals. Head shaking, scratching at the ears, and a black, crusty discharge in the ears characterizes infestation with this mite. "Hot spots" may even appear under and around the ears because of intense scratching. Special miticides (topical medications designed to kill mites) applied into the ears are effective at clearing up most cases of ear mites. Depending upon which miticide is used, a single treatment (ivermectin-based products) or daily treatments (thiabendazole and other acaricides) for four to six weeks may be required to completely rid your pet of these mites. While treating the ears, use a pyrethrin-type flea spray or shampoo on your pet's coat weekly to kill any ear mites that may have climbed out of the ears and sought refuge there.

Allergies

An allergy is caused by the body's immune system overreacting to the presence of foreign protein substances called *allergens*, either on the surface of the body or within the body itself. Common allergens affecting dogs and cats include flea saliva, pollens, dust, fungi, and food-borne proteins. The severity of allergic reactions will vary according to each individual case, yet the outcome is always the same: a very uncomfortable pet!

The most common types of allergies seen in dogs and cats include inhalant allergies (atopy), contact allergies, flea allergies, and food allergies.

Inhalant Allergies

It is estimated that more than 15 percent of all dogs suffer from inhalant allergies, known also as *atopy* or *atopic dermatitis.* Atopy can develop at any age, although 70 percent of the cases develop when the pet is one to three years old. Face rubbing, chewing at the feet, and scratching around the flanks and armpits are the most frequent signs seen with this disorder. Small red bumps, called *papules,* may appear on the skin surface in some cases. Affected pets will often scratch and chew so much that hair loss and secondary skin infection results, leading to even more itching. Inflammation and infections of the ears are commonly seen with atopy as well.

Allergies to grasses, weeds, trees, and shrubs often come and go with the seasons, whereas allergies to house dust, dander, hair, and fungi may be year-round problems. Diagnosis of atopy in pets is based on history and clinical signs, as well as allergy testing. This testing involves either injecting special preparations of the suspected offending agents into the skin and monitoring the skin for a localized allergic response, or testing blood serum samples for antibodies against the various allergens. Regardless of the testing method used, once atopy is diagnosed, treatment can be frustrating because it is highly unlikely that you will be able to completely avoid or

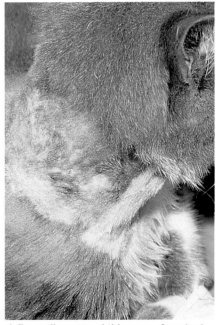

A flea collar caused this case of contact allergy.

Comparison of Inhalant Allergies (Atopy) and Food Allergies

Inhalant Allergies	Food Allergies
Seasonal	Nonseasonal
Responsive to corticosteroids	Nonresponsive to corticosteroids
Nonresponsive to food allergy trial	Responsive to food allergy trial
Gastrointestinal signs rare	Gastrointestinal signs more common

eliminate the offending allergen(s) from your pet's environment.

Traditionally, corticosteroids have been used to reduce the inflammation and itching caused by inhalant allergies, but the continuous, long-term use of these steroids can have serious adverse effects on a pet's health, including skin infections, weight gain, digestive upsets, increased water consumption, and increased urination frequency.

Desensitizing allergy injections, which consist of extracts containing those substances to which the patient is actually allergic, certainly provide safer alternatives to corticosteroids, but in some cases may not be as effective and may take months for favorable results.

Recent Advancements in the Treatment of Atopy

In recent years, several new steroid-free modes of therapy designed to reduce the clinical signs caused by atopy have been studied and implemented with promising results in pets. The first couples antihistamine medications with omega fatty acids (see "Fatty Acids," page 12). Clinical results reveal that this combination can significantly reduce atopic itching and chewing in certain pets. Best of all, both types of medications are safe and inexpensive.

Colloidal oatmeal conditioners can also provide nice topical relief to itchy skin caused by allergies. The conditioner can be diluted in filtered water and applied as a spray (followed by brushing) on a daily basis, thereby providing an ongoing source of itch relief, plus keeping the hair coat clean and smelling nice.

Finally, the drug cyclosporine A is available in capsule form for the treatment of atopy in pets. This compound works by blocking the production of inflammation-inducing chemicals by certain white blood cells within the body, thereby reducing clinical signs associated with the allergy. As with corticosteroids, the dose administered is usually tapered off over several weeks to a maintenance dose that can be administered every other day or even twice weekly.

Contact Allergies

Contact allergies occur when the skin comes in direct contact with an allergen. Plants, plastic bowls, carpets, shampoos, chemical cleaners, and flea collars are all common offenders. Other major offenders include cedar, pine, and/or certain synthetic bedding materials on which the pet may sleep or lie. Because of the nature of the allergy, those areas most affected include the nose, face, feet, and belly. The signs seen with contact allergies are similar to those of inhalant allergies, and differentiating the two can often be difficult. With contact allergies, removing the offending agent or substance will eliminate the condition. In the case of chemicals, sprays, and other topical products, thorough rinsing with water should be performed. If the feet are involved, care must be taken to keep the affected skin dry to prevent an infection from becoming established. If the pet's bedding is suspect, switch to all-cotton bedding materials.

Flea Allergies

Flea allergy dermatitis is different from flea bite dermatitis in that with the latter the itching and irritation occurs at the actual site of the bite. In the case of a flea allergy, however, the saliva of the flea acts as the allergen and can cause an allergic response anywhere on the body. As previously indicated, lesions in dogs typically start on the back near the base of the tail and on the inner hind legs. From there, they can spread forward. In cats, miliary (seedlike) crusts are commonly found around the head and neck. Obviously, the best way to treat such an allergy is to control the fleas on the pet and in the environment (see "Fleas," page 74), and to control any secondary skin infection.

Food Allergies

Food allergies are blamed for many itchy dogs and cats, yet in reality they account for only a small percentage of the "allergies" seen by veterinarians. Signs of a food allergy are the same as those seen with other allergies (that is, itching and hair loss), but with some cases gastrointestinal disturbances, such as excessive gas, vomiting, and diarrhea, may also be present. In cats, miliary dermatitis (see "Miliary Dermatitis," page 105) may appear, marked by intense itching and scabbing around the face and head.

The most common allergy-causing culprits found in commercial dog foods include beef, dairy products, corn, and wheat. Food allergies in cats most often result when diets containing beef, dairy products, and/or fish are consumed. Food allergies can appear at any age, yet approximately 30 percent of cases occur before a pet's first birthday. For this reason, a food allergy should be suspected anytime a pet under one year of age is experiencing itchy skin.

It may take months or years for a pet to develop an allergy to its food, as the body needs time to produce the antibodies that trigger the allergic reaction. Oftentimes, owners complain that their pet developed symptoms of a food allergy immediately after they switched pet food brands. In these instances, a food allergy is not to blame. Instead, a food intolerance has occurred. Food intolerance is not an allergic reaction to protein sources within the food, but a direct reaction to toxins and impurities contained within a ration, and warrants a switch back to the diet that was fed previously.

Diagnosis of a food allergy can be frustrating because it involves food trials, which are usually conducted over 8 to 10 weeks in an attempt to uncover the offending allergen. Rations fed during these trials consist of novel protein diets (diets containing unusual protein sources, such as fish and potato, duck and potato, duck and pea, kangaroo and oat, salmon or whitefish and rice [dogs], or rice and egg) or diets containing protein hydrolysates, which are protein molecules that have been chopped or predigested into smaller protein building blocks that won't cause an allergic response.

If the pet's condition improves on the new ration, its old ration is slowly reintroduced to see whether or not the clinical signs reappear. If they do within two weeks, then a definitive diagnosis of a food allergy can be made and the pet should remain on the special diet for the rest of its life.

Other Types of Allergic Responses

Apart from inhalant, flea, contact, or food allergies, dogs and cats can experience less common forms of allergic reactions that can manifest themselves on the skin.

Type I Hypersensitivity Reactions. Type I hypersensitivity reactions are typically characterized by the formation of hives, or urticaria. These are small, raised patches of skin and hair (wheals) that appear all over the body or, in some instances, are localized to one particular region. Intense itching always accompanies their formation. The presence of hives indicates that an acute allergic reaction of some sort has taken place. This sometimes occurs after an insect sting or vaccination. Because allergic reactions such as these can be serious if swelling occurs around the face and neck, veterinary advice should be sought at once. Antihistamines and/or anti-inflammatory medications are required to control these reactions.

Allergic Reactions to Drugs and Medications. Allergies to drugs have been known to occur and should be considered whenever a dermatopathy appears concurrently with the administration of a medication given either by mouth or injection. Although signs associated with these allergic reactions can be quite variable, including severe gastrointestinal upset and breathing difficulties, many are characterized by intense itching and, in some instances, hair loss at the site of injection. Again, antihistamines and/or anti-inflammatory medications are required to control these reactions, along with discontinuation of the offending medication.

Bacterial Hypersensitivity

Bacterial hypersensitivity is somewhat like an allergy, except that it is not caused by something inhaled, eaten, or touched. Instead, it is caused by an exaggerated immune reaction to the bacteria that normally reside on the skin surface. This condition is much more prevalent in dogs than in cats, and can be made worse by the presence of any of the other allergies mentioned previously. These hypersensitivities are characterized by small pustules and/or circular patches of hair loss caused by folliculitis distributed over the entire coat (see "Folliculitis," page 92). In fact, this condition can be easily mistaken for a case of ringworm if diagnostic tests are not performed. Many dogs suffering from this type of allergy also have an underlying thyroid disorder; therefore, a thyroid test should always be included in the veterinary diagnostic evaluation.

Treatment for this dermatopathy is similar to that for folliculitis: antibiotics, topical medications and shampoos, and anti-inflammatory medication. Other medications, such as thyroid hormone supplements, may be indicated as well. In especially severe cases, administering desensitizing allergy injections consisting of killed preparations of the offending bacteria or parts of the same may help. Regardless of which treatments are used, this is a difficult disorder to control because of the nature of the immune system activity. Recurrences are common, and treatment may need to be provided indefinitely.

Autoimmune Skin Diseases

Like allergies, autoimmune diseases are caused by overreactive immune systems. The difference is that with allergies, the body is allergic to some outside allergen; with autoimmune disease, the body is actually "allergic" to its own tissues, which can include the skin.

In dogs and cats, *pemphigus* is the term used to describe a series of autoimmune diseases that affect the skin. These are characterized by reddened ulcerations and blisters that can be found anywhere on the body, especially around the mouth, lips, and nose. These lesions may or may not be itchy, but they are usually quite painful.

Other autoimmune diseases affecting the skin do exist, but the incidence of occurrence is infrequent. Diagnosis of an autoimmune disease requires a skin biopsy and laboratory evaluation. If one is diagnosed, treatment most often consists of high dosages of steroids or special chemotherapy agents in an attempt to modulate the immune system's activity. Obviously, when treating with such potent medications, close veterinary supervision is essential.

Ringworm and Other Fungal Infections

Ringworm, known as *dermatophytosis,* is not a worm at all; it is a fungus that attacks the skin, hair, and sometimes even the nails of both dogs and cats. A circular patch of hair loss with or without secondary skin infection is the classic lesion seen with this parasitic disease in dogs. In cats, it often presents as miliary dermatitis (see "Miliary Dermatitis," page 105). Yet keep in mind that this clinical manifestation does not occur in every case. In fact, cats and ringworm are so well adapted to each other that felines may not show apparent signs of infection. Thus,

Ringworm affecting the nose of this cat.

undetected ringworm can spread to other pets in the household, and to people as well. In addition, dogs and cats can become infected with ringworm from dirt and soil; therefore, contact with an infected animal is not always needed for transmission.

Because of its potential for causing disease in humans, ringworm must always be suspected as a cause of hair loss in dogs and cats. An examination and/or fungal culture can verify or eliminate such suspicions. Treatment of ringworm is accomplished through the use of whole-body shaves, topical antifungal medications and shampoos, environmental decontamination, and/or oral medications, such as griseofulvin or lufenuron. Be prepared to spend some time with this condition, because some cases can take six to eight weeks, sometimes longer, to resolve.

Unfortunately, ringworm is not the only type of fungus that can affect pets' skin. Though their occurrence is somewhat uncommon, other, more serious types of fungus can infect the skin of dogs and cats. This skin involvement is usually characterized by the formation of firm nodules (see "Lumps or Masses on or Beneath the Skin," page 101) or by ulcerated, draining lesions. To make matters worse, these fungi simultaneously can attack the internal organs of the host and do considerable damage if not detected early. Prompt treatment with a proper antifungal medication is needed for satisfactory recovery in these cases.

Malassezia Dermatitis

Malassezia is the name given to a type of yeast that is normally found on the skin of otherwise healthy dogs and cats. However, if the skin of these pets becomes inflamed because of allergies, cornification disorders, or autoimmune disease, this yeast can begin to proliferate and colonize the skin in great numbers, aggravating the existing skin disease. Pets afflicted with *Malassezia* dermatitis can experience enhanced itching, scaling, and redness of the skin. In addition, the skin will emit a characteristic musty odor, and will be greasy or waxy to the touch. Areas most commonly affected are the ears, underside of the neck, belly, inner thighs, paws, and anywhere there is skin-to-skin contact.

Breeds predisposed to *Malassezia* overgrowth include West Highland White Terriers, German Shepherds, Shih Tzus, Basset Hounds, and Dachshunds. Fortunately, *Malassezia* dermatitis is rare in cats.

Veterinarians typically diagnose this type of dermatitis by pressing a slide against the affected skin, staining it, then examining it for yeast organisms under the microscope. A cotton swab may also be used to collect a sample from the ears and/or between the toes.

Treatment for *Malassezia* dermatitis can be challenging because the organisms are normally found on the skin. The underlying disease that led

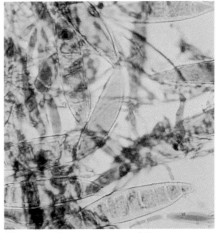

Microscopic appearance of the ringworm organism.

to the dermatitis in the first place needs to be addressed, and then efforts need to be made to reduce the yeast population to such a level as to eliminate the clinical signs associated with it. This can be accomplished with medicated shampoos (containing miconazole, selenium, or chlorhexidine) and, for tough cases, oral antifungal medications.

Bacterial Skin Infections

Bacterial skin infections rarely arise spontaneously in dogs and cats, but rather are more likely to appear secondarily to another condition. For example, physical or chemical trauma (wounds and abrasions), parasitism (such as fleas and mange), abnormal immune response (allergies, pemphigus), or even normal anatomy (skin-fold infections on the face and nose) can all predispose the skin to infections. Every dog and cat has a resident population of bacteria that naturally resides on the skin, usually without causing any problems whatsoever. However, when the normal health and integrity of the skin are disrupted, disease-causing bacteria can multiply and outnumber the resident bacteria. When this happens, infections can gain a foothold.

In addition to a number of causes, bacterial skin infections can assume a number of appearances. *Pyoderma* is the term used to describe those skin infections that have pus (dead blood cells and tissue debris) as one of their features. Other infections may not have any pus, but may instead be characterized by many small scabs and crusts. Still others may appear as hair loss only, with little evidence of skin involvement. Recognizing which type of bacterial infection is involved is crucial because treatment regimens can vary widely depending on the type.

There are many medicated shampoos from which to choose to treat skin infections (see the table on page 28). Some require a prescription; others do not. If you plan to use a nonprescription shampoo, be certain to select the right one. Shampoos containing chlorhexidine, triclosan, or povidone iodine are effective at fighting infections. (Note: Because most cats are sensitive to iodine products, these should be avoided in lieu of the other formula-

tions.) Benzoyl peroxide is also a very effective ingredient against skin infections, yet few shampoos containing this chemical are available without a prescription from your veterinarian. Proper selection is vital, so ask your veterinarian for advice.

Pet owners should never attempt to treat major infections, such as those extending beneath the outer surface of the skin and accompanied by bleeding, or superficial infections that involve extensive areas of the skin surface, at home. These need to be evaluated and treated by your veterinarian as soon as possible. This is true also for those seemingly minor infections that fail to resolve within a day or two. Specially formulated medicated shampoos; antibiotic, antifungal, and/or anti-inflammatory medications; or injections are required to treat these infections and prevent any undesirable aftereffects. Some cases may require surgical intervention before the healing process can be effected.

Hot Spots

A "hot spot," or acute moist dermatitis, is nothing more than a swollen, moist, raw area of bacterial infection on the skin. Traditionally, this term has been restricted to dogs, yet theoretically, cats can develop hot spots as well. The telltale signs associated with these moist lesions are intense itching and rapid spread of the moist infection over the skin surface. You must be alert for signs of spreading. What starts out as a quarter-sized hot spot below the ear of a dog can spread over the entire neck and forequarters in only a matter of hours. In addition, unless you can prevent your pet from licking or scratching, these actions too will aggravate the condition further by keeping the infection moist and irritating the skin.

What causes hot spots? Most of the time, fleas or allergies are to blame, but anything that irritates the skin can be suspect. For instance, ear mites and ear infections can play a leading role in the development of hot spots around the head and ears. Usually the irritation caused by these dermatopathies or parasites induce the pet to chew, lick, or scratch at the affected sites. Once the skin becomes injured by these actions and the traumatized areas accumulate moisture through oozing blood and serum and through licking, an infection follows. Once the infection becomes established, the irritation intensifies, and the licking, chewing, and scratching follow suit. A vicious cycle develops.

Dogs and cats with long coats or heavy undercoats develop hot spots more readily than others do. In addition, pets that have been moved from northern, cooler climates into hot southern climates are prime candidates. Breed predispositions can occur as well, with Labrador Retrievers and Golden Retrievers leading the list.

Treatment for hot spots should first be directed at drying the affected areas, followed by treating the infection itself. Clipping the hair

from the affected regions provides an excellent way to allow air to circulate and help with the drying process. Don't worry about how your pet will look after the clipping; the hair will grow back! One word of caution: Because these lesions are often extremely painful, tranquilization and professional restraint may be needed before clipping can be performed safely.

A drying agent should be applied directly to the moist lesions. Avoid using alcohol for this purpose, because you are liable to get bitten. As an alternative, you can use your pet's ear-cleaning solution. These solutions are designed as drying agents and are effective weapons against moist infections. Other so-called "hot spot" remedies, most of which contain a drying substance plus an antimicrobial agent such as sulfur, may or may not be effective

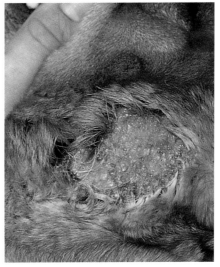

Acute moist dermatitis.

91

against tough lesions, so consult your veterinarian first before using such products.

Regardless of the drying agent used, it should be applied four to six times daily to be effective—more often if your pet has the propensity to lick. In addition, after each application of drying solution, a triple antibiotic cream or ointment can be spread over the lesion to enhance healing. (A triple antibiotic preparation is one that is compounded of three different antibiotics in a spreadable medium.) Finally, an Elizabethan collar (E-collar) or another similar restraint device worn around the neck may be needed to prevent the pet from licking and chewing at the lesions during the healing process.

For hot spots that encompass a large area or are actively spreading, antibiotics and anti-inflammatory medications are a must. Don't waste time trying to treat these at home. The sooner you get medical attention, the sooner you'll resolve the problem.

Skin-Fold Pyoderma (Intertrigo)

Some dogs and cats are prone to moist skin infections simply because of their anatomy. Skin-fold infections are a good example of this. Redundant folds of skin lead to poor air circulation within these areas, creating a warm, dark, moist environment, ideal for bacterial growth. For example, breeds with deep skin folds around their nose and eyes, such as Pugs and Persian cats, are highly susceptible to nasal-fold infections. Pyodermas involving lip folds often appear in Cocker Spaniels and similar breeds, and can significantly add to the "bad breath" that many owners of these pets complain about. Similarly, dogs that have curly tails, such as Boston Terriers, may have this problem in the skin folds surrounding the tail.

The objectives for treatment of skin-fold pyoderma are to clear up any infection present and to maintain a dry environment within the affected areas. The first objective can be met by cleaning the affected areas daily with medicated shampoos or gels containing 2.5 percent benzoyl peroxide, then applying a drying agent (see "Hot Spots," page 90) to the skin between the folds. Once the initial infection has been resolved, periodic application (three to four times weekly) of the drying agent will help prevent recurrence. In difficult or recurring cases, cosmetic surgery, aimed at the removal of the offending skin folds, can be helpful.

Folliculitis

Folliculitis is the term given to any bacterial infection involving the hair follicles. The hallmark signs of folliculitis include the presence of numerous scabs and crusts, and/or small pustules, some of which may have tiny hairs extending from their centers. Pets suffering from folliculitis may actually look as though they have a bad case of hives. And, as you might expect, whenever the hair follicles are involved, hair loss usually follows soon after. As a result, the hair coats of dogs and cats afflicted with folliculitis are often "moth-eaten" in appearance.

Oral antibiotics combined with medicated shampoos containing povidone iodine, triclosan, chlorhexidine, or 2.5 percent benzoyl peroxide are frequently used to treat folliculitis in dogs and cats. Daily application of medicated skin and coat sprays, containing similar ingredients, is also an effective part of any treatment program.

Impetigo

Impetigo, also known as *puppy pyoderma,* typically affects puppies under six months of age. Characterized by the presence of numerous small pustules on the belly, inner legs, and armpits, impetigo is often incorrectly mistaken for ant or mosquito bites. Fortunately, this is one disease that pet owners needn't worry too much about. In most cases, the use of medicated shampoos is the only treatment needed. In some instances, the infection clears up spontaneously without any treatment at all. Recurrences of impetigo are rare as the puppy matures.

Juvenile Pyoderma

As with impetigo, juvenile pyoderma, also known as *puppy strangles,* occurs in puppies less than six months of age. But unlike the former disease, this dermatopathy can be a serious disease if left untreated. This type of infection localizes around the

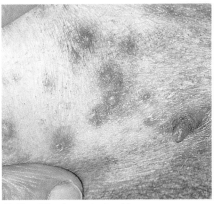

Folliculitis characterized by numerous pustules, scabs, and crusts.

lips, eyelids, and ears of affected puppies, and often causes generalized facial swelling. In addition, enlargement of the lymph nodes in the neck usually accompanies episodes of juvenile pyoderma. Unless prompt therapy consisting of antibiotics and steroids is obtained, unsightly, irreversible scarring can be an unfortunate consequence of this disease.

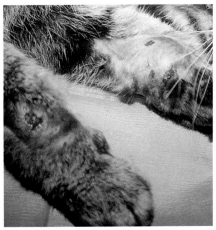

Bite wounds at the site of an abscess.

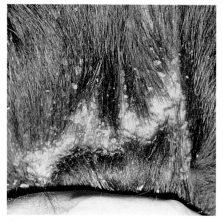

Seborrhea sicca.

Abscesses and Cellulitis

Both of these terms refer to bacterial infections that involve the deeper layers of the skin or underlying tissues. The difference between the two lies in the fact that true abscesses have distinct, defined boundaries, whereas cellulitis claims no boundaries. Pain and swelling are distinct features of both, and pus-draining tracts are often seen with the former. (Always wear gloves if handling a pet with a draining tract until a diagnosis can be made. Fungal organisms, most of which are highly contagious to humans, could be responsible. See page 88.) These dermatopathies are among the most common causes of fever, depression, and loss of appetite in cats. Normally resulting from bite wounds acquired during fighting, feline abscesses arise most often on the face, on the back near the base of the tail, and on the legs. In fact, abscesses should be suspected whenever a cat comes home limping.

Abscesses and cellulitis in dogs and cats warrant prompt veterinary attention. Because they involve the deeper layers of the skin, septicemia (blood poisoning) could result if neglected. If this happens, the infection could then spread to the internal organs, including the heart and kidneys. To prevent this, treatment should include high dosages of antibiotics and, if necessary, surgical drainage of the abscess.

Pododermatitis (Interdigital Pyoderma)

Dermatopathies involving the feet of dogs and cats can be frustrating to deal with because they can result from a number of sources. For example, allergies, parasites (such as mange and ringworm), foreign bodies (for example, grass burrs), ingrown hairs, and trauma (both physical and chemical) have all been implicated at one time or another. Dogs and cats kept in wet, unsanitary environments also are prone to developing this affliction. One possible way to separate the causes is to determine how many feet are affected. If just one foot is involved, trauma, parasites, or foreign bodies could be to blame. On the other hand, if multiple feet are affected, the source could be allergies or filthy environmental conditions. In most cases of pododermatitis, incessant licking and moist bacterial infections accompany the lesions.

After addressing the source of the pododermatitis, the infection should be treated by soaking the affected feet for 15 minutes, three to four times daily, in solutions containing chlorhexidine or triclosan. After soaking, the feet and toes should be dried thoroughly using a blow-dryer or by applying some type of drying agent, such as an ear-cleansing solution.

Diseases of Cornification (Seborrhea)

Diseases of cornification is a general term used to describe a series of conditions characterized by abnormal skin cell growth and turnover with or without abnormal sebaceous gland activity (see "The Skin," page 7). Such disorders will result in skin that is either excessively flaky or excessively greasy, depending on which disease is involved. Primary diseases of cornification usually restrict themselves to dogs, with the exception of "stud tail" in cats (see "Stud Tail," page 105). Those canine breeds with noted predispositions include Doberman Pinschers, Irish Setters, Cocker Spaniels, and Springer Spaniels. Disruptions in the cornification process can also occur in both dogs and cats alike in response to some external or internal disturbance, including hormonal imbalances, allergies, nutritional deficiencies, skin parasites, and skin infections.

Seborrhea is a common disease of cornification seen by veterinarians.

Dandruff-like flakes of skin resulting from abnormal skin cell turnover characterize the dry form of seborrhea, called *seborrhea sicca*. Doberman Pinschers are especially predisposed to this type of flaking, which can appear in great abundance all over the coat—much to the dismay of their owners. Itching may or may not be a factor in these cases. In contrast to seborrhea sicca, *seborrhea oleosa* is characterized by excess sebum production by the sebaceous glands. This makes the skin and coat excessively greasy and oily, and oftentimes leaves it inflamed and reeking with a bad odor. Secondary skin infections and itching are common with seborrhea oleosa.

In cases of cornification defects caused by other disease conditions, diagnosis and treatment of the underlying cause is needed to clear it up. Other treatment methods useful

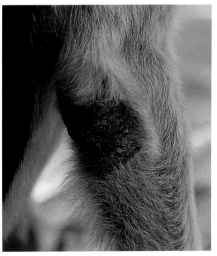

Elbow hygroma.

for both primary and secondary cornification diseases include daily dietary supplementation with balanced vitamin, mineral, and fatty acid preparations; weekly anti-seborrhea shampoos; and, in the case of seborrhea sicca, daily application of moisturizing and emollient rinses or sprays. Brushing the coat at least twice a day is beneficial therapy as well.

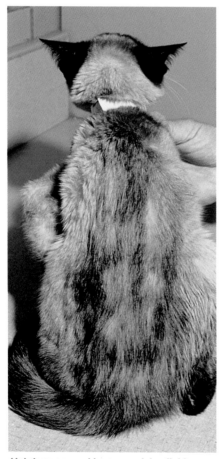

Hair loss caused by compulsive licking.

Skin Calluses

Seen primarily on the elbows, lower hind legs, and other pressure points that contact hard surfaces, calluses are certainly unsightly, yet normally pose no health threat. Sometimes, however, they can become infected and may need to be medicated. Because lying on hard surfaces causes calluses, this factor needs to be addressed. If your porch or patio is concrete, provide carpeting, blankets, or towels on which your dog can lie. Soft bedding within doghouses will also ease the irritation placed on these pressure points. The calluses can be treated with skin moisturizers, petroleum jelly, and/or lanolin applied three to four times daily. These agents will help soften the calluses and stimulate new hair growth. Daily application of creams containing vitamin E and lanolin have proven to be helpful in selected cases as well.

Neurodermatitis

Neurodermatitis refers to those skin conditions that can be seen in pets that are excessively nervous or excitable, or those pets suffering from emotional distress because of their environments. In dogs, a common form of neurodermatitis is *acral lick dermatitis*. In cats, neurodermatitis is also known as *hyperesthesia syndrome*.

Acral lick dermatitis is identified by constant licking or chewing at an isolated region of the skin, usually somewhere on the legs. Quite often the area in question becomes thickened, raw, and ulcerated, with secondary infections by bacteria common. Boredom is thought to play a leading role in this disease; for lack of a better explanation, the dog has "nothing better to do." In some instances, local inflammation of nerve endings, resulting from previous injuries or trauma to the site(s), or hypothyroidism (see "Thyroid Hormone," page 98) may be contributing factors.

Treatment of acral lick dermatitis consists of local application of medicated creams and ointments to help soothe the inflammation and prevent infection. Injections of anti-inflammatory drugs directly into the lesions may also be helpful. If boredom or some other underlying factor is involved, that needs to be addressed as well.

Hyperesthesia syndrome in cats classically presents itself as biting, scratching, and/or licking at the back, tail, inner thighs, and belly for no apparent reason, leaving broken, thinned hair in these regions and oftentimes a classic "stripe" of broken hair down the middle of the back. Infection may or may not be present. More than 90 percent of the time, the more "emotional" feline breeds— Siamese, Burmese, Abyssinian, and Himalayan—are involved. These breeds seem most likely to use their tongues as their means of releasing stress, and as every cat owner knows, a cat's tongue is more effec-tive at removing hair than the fanciest slicker brush!

As mentioned above, emotional upset, caused by changes in household routine, the addition of a new pet into the house, or just simply being left alone, is usually the triggering factor for this dermatopathy. Because of this behavioral component, this condition can be difficult to treat. Eliminating the cause of the emotional stress is certainly the first place to start. Try to identify any changes that may have taken place in your or your cat's daily routine and, if possible, get them back to the way they were. If you have recently brought a new puppy or kitten into the household, are you inadvertently ignoring your older friend? If so, try giving your older pet some extra attention. It may solve the problem. Likewise, if your cat gets upset when you leave, try leaving on the television or radio while you are gone. Little details such as these must be addressed to reduce the stress that is causing the behavior.

In addition to the measures mentioned above, feline pheromone therapy has also been used with varying degrees of success to combat this disorder. When sprayed or released into a cat's immediate environment, these pheromones can exert a calming effect on an otherwise nervous cat, making the cat less likely to lick indiscriminately. Be sure to ask your veterinarian about this novel approach to therapy, which has proved useful for discouraging urine marking and destructive scratching as well.

Finally, daily brushing is a must for these cats. Not only will this help remove any dead hair present and stimulate regrowth, but it will provide your pet with some added attention that may prove to be curative in itself.

Hormone-Related Dermatopathies

Hormones are compounds that control and modify specific functions within the body. Because their presence is so vital, it is easy to see how too much or too little of a specific hormone could upset the delicate balance within the body and lead to illness.

Because a healthy skin and coat are always in an active, dynamic state of growth and regeneration, abnormal changes in the blood levels of certain hormones cannot help but manifest themselves outwardly as dermatopathies. These hormones include thyroid hormones, steroid hormones, and insulin. When one or more of these hormones is present in abnormal amounts, the integument may show signs of symmetrical hair loss and increased pigmentation (darkening) of the skin. Itching is rarely a feature. Although these outward changes may be the first signs of a problem detected by a pet owner, closer scrutiny will often reveal other signs of illness—signs having nothing to do with the skin and coat.

Thyroid Hormone

Because thyroid hormone is responsible for regulating overall body and skin metabolism, hypothyroidism (low levels of thyroid hormone) has a profound effect on the skin and coat. This disorder is usually seen only in dogs, with breeds such as Doberman Pinschers, Dachshunds, Golden Retrievers, and Cocker Spaniels affected the most. Canines suffering from this disorder tend to have thinned hair coats, including loss of the soft undercoats. The skin appears thicker than normal, and may have increased pigmentation. Seborrhea may occur, which could lead to itching. Affected dogs will tire easily, and may accumulate excess weight. Ear infections are often seen with hypothyroidism.

The causes of hypothyroidism are complicated and beyond the scope of this discussion, yet the diagnosis and treatment are not. Veterinarians have the ability to perform preliminary in-house blood tests to determine thyroid levels in pets suspected of having this disorder. If found positive for hypothyroidism, follow-up tests may be performed on the patient to confirm the diagnosis and to determine the actual extent of the problem. Treatment of hypothyroidism is not difficult: daily oral supplementation of thyroid hormone. In most cases, the medication must be given for the rest of the pet's life to prevent recurrences.

If hypothyroidism seems to limit itself to dogs, naturally occurring hyperthyroidism (high levels of thyroid hormone) does the same for cats. Too much of this hormone results in weight loss, a voracious appetite, and unkempt, greasy coats, among other signs. Hyperthyroidism in cats is caused by cancer of the thyroid gland, and can be treated with chemotherapy, radioactive iodine therapy, or surgical removal of the malignant gland. Oversupplementation of thyroid hormone to dogs can also result in signs of hyperthyroidism in this species; reducing the levels administered resolves the problem swiftly.

Steroid Hormones

Steroid hormones serve more than 40 different functions within the body—all of vital importance. The body produces many types of steroid hormones. In regard to the skin and coat, we are not concerned with the body-building types (anabolic steroids), but with a special group called *glucocorticosteroids*. Some familiar names within this classification include cortisone, prednisone, and prednisolone. Among their many functions, the one that stands out in both veterinary and human medicine is their ability to reduce inflammation. Dogs and cats are given these steroids to stop itching, relieve pain, prevent shock, and reduce inflammation caused by a wide variety of injuries or illnesses. Used appropriately, they are effective weapons that induce much-

needed relief for pets suffering from dermatopathies.

If glucocorticosteroids are so helpful, then why not use them all the time? Glucocorticosteroids, when given steadily over a long period of time, can have some very undesirable, even life-threatening, side effects. Providing the body with a continuous supply of oral, injectable, or topical (creams and ointments) steroids may impair the animal's own ability to produce these compounds naturally, which could have fatal consequences if these outside steroid sources are ever discontinued. Furthermore, chronically high levels of steroid hormones within the body can eventually cause secondary Cushing's disease (see below), as well as suppress the body's immune system, leaving the dog or cat prone to other diseases, including cancer. As a result, the use of steroids to treat your pet's skin condition should be under the direct supervision of your veterinarian.

High levels of glucocorticosteroids within the body can also be caused by a disease that affects the adrenal glands, the organs that normally produce a variety of steroid compounds within the body. This condition is known as *Cushing's disease,* and is more common in dogs than it is in cats. Pets with Cushing's disease display observable changes in the skin and coat, as well as in the other body systems. These changes can include thinning of the skin, seborrhea, increased pigmentation, and secondary bacterial infections. The hair is usually dry and brittle, and thin on both sides of the body. Signs unrelated to the skin often include a loss of muscle mass (resulting in a "potbellied" appearance), increased urination, and excessive panting.

Blood tests are required to confirm this disease in pets. Cancer is the cause of primary Cushing's disease (as mentioned above, secondary Cushing's can result from long-term treatment with glucocorticosteroids). As a result, therapy includes either surgery or chemotherapy to reduce the secretion of hormones.

Insulin

Insulin is the hormone produced by the body that works to facilitate the transfer of glucose from the bloodstream to the cells within the body, thereby providing those cells with a source of energy. Diabetes mellitus is a disease characterized by a decreased production of insulin by the body, or by an impaired response to the insulin that is produced. This, in turn, leads to decreased absorption of glucose from the bloodstream by the cells. Because these body cells cannot use the glucose for energy, they must draw on other sources of energy, such as protein and fat, to supply their energy needs. Unfortunately, this protein and fat can be drawn from the integument, leading to symmetrical hair loss, cornification defects, and secondary bacterial skin infections. Other non-skin-related signs of diabetes mellitus include weight loss, increased urination, and cataracts. Obviously, identifying and treating the diabetes affords relief from its related dermatopathies and other complications.

Acne

Acne is a skin condition characterized by bumps, pustules, and/or blackheads on the chin of affected dogs and cats. The cause of acne has yet to be determined, but some think inadequate self-grooming in this area may be a big factor. Regardless, problems such as mange, ringworm, and so on, must be ruled out before settling with a diagnosis of acne. Treatment for acne includes a thorough daily scrubbing with a mild, antibacterial soap or 2.5 percent benzoyl peroxide shampoo, followed by application of a drying agent (such as ear cleanser). This should eliminate the problem. In really difficult cases, antibiotics may be required for a complete cure.

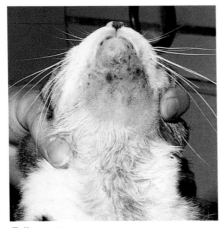

Feline acne.

Lumps or Masses on or Beneath the Skin

Any lump or bump found on or beneath the skin of your pet warrants immediate attention. Oftentimes, the first thought that comes to mind is tumor, but that is not always the case. If felt beneath the skin, the lump could indeed be a tumor, but it could also be a cyst, abscess, or area of chronic inflammation called a *granuloma*. If the mass is actually protruding from the skin, more than likely it is either a granuloma or a tumor (including warts). Do not rely on your interpretive abilities. Have the mass examined immediately by your veterinarian because, if it indeed turns out to be something serious, early detection means greater chances for a complete recovery.

Tumors involving the skin and underlying tissues can be either malignant (cancerous) or benign (noncancerous). The only way to differentiate the two is by the microscopic examination of a sample taken from the tumor. To the naked eye, tumors can take on a wide variety of shapes and forms, from obvious, firm masses on or beneath the skin to raised, ulcerated lesions that may be easily mistaken for a hot spot or some similar dermatopathy. If you detect an abnormal mass, an abnormal pigment change, or any lesion slow to heal that involves your pet's skin, it could be cancer. Take

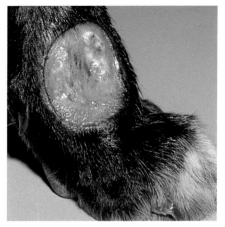

A skin tumor affecting the paw.

your pet to the veterinarian for an examination promptly.

A lipoma is a type of benign tumor that occurs frequently in dogs and therefore deserves special mention. These lumps develop from the fatty tissue just beneath the skin, and can grow to considerable sizes. Older, overweight animals are more likely to develop these than their younger, leaner peers. Often these masses can be diagnosed in your veterinarian's office by using a needle to withdraw some of the fatty tissue for microscopic examination. Rarely does a lipoma turn malignant; however, if not removed, it should be rechecked periodically to confirm its benign status. Lipomas are rare in cats.

Cysts are round sacs filled with fluid or debris. Sebaceous cysts are probably the most common type of cyst seen involving pets, and they mainly affect dogs. These firm, nodular structures can be found anywhere on the body that sebaceous glands are found (see "The Skin," page 7). Definitive treatment includes surgical removal or cauterization (burning) of the offending cyst.

Unlike cysts, granulomas are solid structures composed mainly of fibrous tissue and inflammatory cells that form in response to foreign bodies, fungal organisms, and certain types of bacteria penetrating the skin or body cavity. For instance, thorns or slivers that penetrate the skin may stimulate this type of reaction. What the body is actually trying to do in these instances is to form a protective covering around the unwelcome foreign body, thereby effectively isolating it. Over time, this protective covering can harden and become noticeable to the touch. Again, diagnosis is made by microscopic examination of the affected tissue.

Granulomas have also been associated with vaccination reactions, resulting in a lump forming at the site where a vaccination was given. In most cases, no treatment is needed for these, as these granulomas will eventually resolve on their own. However, for most others, surgical removal may be necessary if their size and/or location warrant removal.

Warts (papillomas) are familiar to all of us. Any breed of dog or cat can be affected by these cauliflower-like growths. Warts can show up on the eyelids, in the mouth, or anywhere else on the body, including the feet. Some originate from the sebaceous glands of the skin; others develop from the epidermis itself. Regardless of their origin, they are usually benign in nature, and pose no threat to health. Some warts can get so large that they become traumatized and ulcerated, predisposing them to infection. In these cases, surgical removal under a local anesthetic provides the easiest and quickest method of treatment. And just in case the idea crosses your mind, do not use human wart preparations on these warts. Doing so may harm your pet!

Pigment and Color Changes Involving the Skin and Hair

Melanin is the name of the pigment contained within the skin that helps determine skin and coat color in dogs and cats. It also helps protect the skin from the harmful effects of the sun's radiation. Solar dermatitis (see page 104) is a prime example of what insufficient levels of pigment can lead to. Skin cancer can be another unfortunate side effect of poorly pigmented skin exposed to the sun's ultraviolet rays.

Genetics plays an important role in the amount of pigmentation within the skin and hair. Albino dogs and cats are totally devoid of pigment whatsoever. You can imagine how sensitive they are to normal, or even reduced, levels of sunlight. Less dramatic genetic disorders involving melanin can exist as well. Interestingly enough, many of these are associated with deafness in the affected animal. White-haired, blue-eyed deaf cats are good examples of this phenomenon.

Hypopigmentation, or underpigmentation, can result from other factors besides genetics. Any type of trauma to the skin (burns, frostbite, cuts, deep abrasions, and so on) that is deep enough to affect the base of the hair shaft can destroy pigment-producing cells (melanocytes), resulting in a loss of pigmentation at the next hair cycle. Certain inflammatory skin diseases, such as pemphigus (see page 87), may cause hypopigmentation of the affected skin, especially around the lips and nose. Lastly, prolonged exposure to the sun, and, for those pets that enjoy swimming, prolonged exposure to chlorine, can lighten the hair coat as well.

Conversely, hyperpigmentation, or overpigmentation, can have a genetic basis, but its sudden or gradual appearance over time could mean that some underlying disease is to blame. One of the most common causes of spontaneous darkening of the skin and/or hair is inflammation. Long-term exposure to allergens, parasites, and skin infections can gradually lead to hyperpigmentation of the skin. Localized cases of skin hyperpigmentation have been known to appear after the injection of a drug or vaccine.

Increases in skin temperature that accompany these inflammatory

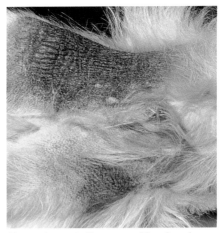
Hyperpigmentation caused by chronic skin inflammation.

processes can also cause a transient darkening of the hair coat, either locally or widespread over the body. In most instances, the normal hair color will return at the next hair cycle.

Other causes of hyperpigmentation can include chronic irritation (licking or rubbing), cancer, and hormone-related dermatopathies such as Cushing's disease and hypothyroidism. As far as cancer is concerned, melanoma (pigmented skin tumor) is one of the most serious types that can affect dogs and cats because it can spread (metastasize) rapidly. Melanomas are usually blue-black or brown in color, and can assume a number of different shapes. Any unexplained areas of hyperpigmentation involving the skin should be suspect and checked out immediately.

Acanthosis nigricans is a hormonal condition seen in Dachshunds, Cocker Spaniels, and certain other breeds, resulting in hair loss, hyper-pigmentation (especially affecting the armpits and chest), and thickened skin that is itchy and greasy. Acanthosis is diagnosed using skin biopsies; treatment is nonspecific, employing corticosteroids to reduce pain and inflammation, aloe vera gel and antiseborrheic products applied topically to affected regions, and, in certain instances, antibiotics.

Solar Dermatitis

Ultraviolet rays from the sun contacting lightly pigmented skin are responsible for this skin disorder, which is also known as *photodermatitis*. In fact, it can be equated to a severe case of sunburn! Reddened, ulcerated sores appearing on the nose and ears are common clinical signs associated with photodermatitis. In addition, chronic solar dermatitis can often lead to skin cancer. Dogs and cats with white coats are predisposed to this disease because of the reduced amounts of protective pigmentation in their skin.

Existing sores should be treated with topical antibiotic creams to control infection. Exposure to the sun's rays needs to be reduced as well. Keeping your pet indoors on sunny days will reduce this exposure. Sunblock or sunscreen with a rating of 15 or higher may be applied directly to the affected areas to block out the ultraviolet rays. They should be reapplied often to ensure maximum effectiveness.

Hair Loss Not Related to Disease

There are a few instances in which lack or loss of hair is not caused by a disease, but by normal genetic or physiological factors. Genetic examples include Mexican Hairless and certain Chihuahua dogs, "blue" Doberman Pinschers and Dachshunds, as well as the normal hair thinning seen on the heads of cats just in front of the ears (preauricular baldness).

One example of a physiological factor is *telogen defluxion*. This complex term refers to hair loss caused by stress. Pregnancy, illness, trauma, and other factors can all cause enough stress on the body to cause this type of hair loss. A simple trip to the veterinary office can induce this as well. Did you ever wonder why your pet sheds so much whenever you take it to the veterinarian? Telogen defluxion is being employed as a defense mechanism. With the loosening of the hair within the hair follicles that occurs, anything that tries to grab an unwilling pet is probably bound to end up with a mouthful (or, in our case, a handful) of hair instead. You might liken the reaction to that of the lizard that loses its tail when threatened.

Another example of a physiological basis for hair loss is the phenomenon in which the normal hair cycle suddenly stops or becomes dormant. Illness or trauma can cause the hair cycle to temporarily come to a halt, leaving no replacement for the dead hair that is eventually shed. This may also be seen when hair is shorn off close to the skin using clippers, as performed before a surgery. In some cases, the hair may take months to grow back.

Dermatopathies Unique to Cats

Miliary Dermatitis

Have you ever found a cluster of tiny crusts or scabs around the neck or head of your cat? If so, you are observing the skin condition known as *feline miliary dermatitis.* Miliary dermatitis actually refers to the unique way a cat's skin reacts to certain irritants or diseases. It is not a disease entity in itself; it is simply a sign of disease. These crusty lesions, which can be found anywhere on the body, are the irritating source of constant licking, rubbing, and scratching. Fleas cause more than 75 percent of the cases of miliary dermatitis. Atopy, ringworm, food allergies, mange, and fatty acid deficiencies are among the other notable causes.

The first step in treating a cat with miliary dermatitis is to identify and treat the dermatopathy that is causing the problem. At the same time, anti-inflammatory drugs and/or antimicrobial medications prescribed by your veterinarian can be used to help relieve the discomfort and extent of the miliary reaction.

Eosinophilic Granuloma Complex

As with feline miliary dermatitis, eosinophilic granuloma complex is merely an outward sign or side effect of another underlying dermatopathy, usually an allergy of some type. Ulcerations on the lips, fire-red bumps or elevations on the belly or inner thighs, or raised, yellow-pink nodules on the back part of the hind legs are the most prevalent signs seen with this complex. Treatment for eosinophilic granuloma complex is essentially the same as that for miliary dermatitis; however, improvement may not come as quickly. Recurrences can and do occur, especially in those instances in which the underlying disorder proves to be difficult to control.

Stud Tail

"Stud tail" is a seborrhea-like skin condition commonly seen in male cats, although females can suffer from it as well. Characterized by a buildup of yellow-black, greasy deposits at the base of the tail, stud tail is caused by hyperactivity of sebaceous glands located in this particular region. Treatment consists of gently cleaning the affected area with a mild soap or shampoo, followed by the application of some type of drying agent, such as isopropyl alcohol or an ear-cleansing solution. As a general rule, treatment should be performed two to three times weekly to help keep this condition under control.

Chapter Eight

First Aid for Grooming Injuries

If you happen to cut your pet's toenail too closely or get soap in your pet's eyes, don't panic. Here are some first aid techniques applicable to these and other situations that you might encounter when grooming your pet. If a serious injury occurs, contact your veterinarian immediately for instructions on any further first aid steps that need to be taken before the trip to the veterinary hospital.

Bleeding Nails

If you are diligent with your home grooming program, no doubt this event will eventually occur. Don't feel bad—your pet will recover! Just stay calm and follow these instructions:

1. Using a clean cloth, tissue, or gauze pad, apply direct pressure to the bleeding end of the nail for 5 to 10 minutes. If you wish, you can even tape a piece of tissue or gauze to the end of the nail.

When accidents happen, the wise home groomer is always prepared with the appropriate first aid supplies and techniques.

2. If available, apply commercially available styptic gel or powder to the end of the affected nail using a cotton-tipped applicator. Reapply as needed. A bar of soap or toothpaste can also be used to "plug" the end of the nail.

Lacerations (Cuts)

The three most common causes of lacerations secondary to grooming are (1) the improper use and care of clipper blades, (2) careless attempts to remove mats and tangles with scissors, and (3) a pet that does not want to be groomed. If such an injury does occur, follow these guidelines:

• If the wound is bleeding profusely, apply direct pressure for a minimum of five minutes, using a sterile gauze pad or clean cloth. Do not try to wash the wound, because this will just aggravate the bleeding. Seek veterinary assistance at once.

• If there is little or no bleeding from the cut or laceration, use a mild hand soap or a chlorhexidine solution to clean the wound. Rinse thoroughly and blot dry, preferably using a sterile gauze pad.

• For minor cuts, apply an antibiotic ointment or cream to the wound three times daily for five to seven days to help prevent infection. Light bandaging is optional, but it may prevent licking or chewing by your pet.

• If at any time signs of infection appear (redness, swelling, heat, and pain), contact your veterinarian.

Clipper Burns

Clipper burn is the term used to describe any injury or irritation caused by the use of electric clippers. Clipper burn can be caused by (1) the actual blades becoming too hot during the clipping procedure and burning the skin; (2) broken teeth on the clipper blade scraping or raking the skin surface, causing abrasions; or (3) dull blades pulling the hairs from their follicles, creating localized inflammation.

Obviously the best way to treat clipper burn is to prevent it in the first place by properly caring for clipper blades. However, if it does happen, take the following steps:

• Gently scrub the region with soap and water, then dry well.

• After drying, apply an antibiotic ointment or cream to the wound three times daily for five to seven days to help prevent infection.

• If the burn seems to be especially bothersome to the pet, over-the-counter preparations containing aloe or topical anesthetics can provide soothing relief when applied three times daily.

If at any time signs of infection appear (redness, swelling, heat, and pain), contact your veterinarian.

Allergic Reactions

Allergic reactions that occur after application of a topical spray or shampoo are normally characterized by intense itching and reddening of the skin. They are rarely life threatening. If an insecticide is involved, however, this is not always the case. Signs associated with this type of poisoning can include vomiting, diarrhea, excessive salivation, and pinpoint pupil size. The presence of any of these signs warrants immediate action. Fortunately, with the advent of a new generation of flea- and tick-control products, the incidence of insecticide-related allergic reactions has decreased dramatically (see page 78).

If you suspect an allergic reaction after the application of a topical spray or shampoo, follow these procedures:

• Rinse your pet thoroughly with water to remove the offending agent. Cold water, combined with a colloidal oatmeal rinse, is an effective anti-itch remedy and should be used if itching is a component of the reaction.

• If the above action fails to provide relief, or if swelling or any other abnormal signs appear, contact your veterinarian immediately. An antihistamine or anti-inflammatory injection may be needed.

In the case of an insecticidal poisoning, follow these procedures:

• Rinse your pet off thoroughly with cool water.

• Seek veterinary help immediately. In most cases, an antidote is available to counteract the harmful effects of the poison. Be certain to take the bottle or package from the offending agent used with you to the veterinary clinic.

Cracked Pads

Although cracked footpads can't exactly be classified as a grooming injury, first aid for this problem in dogs and cats is worth mentioning. Cracked pads can result from contact with hard surfaces, foreign objects such as rocks or glass, and even nutritional deficiencies. Because the pads are composed of a very thick layer of dead epithelial cells, these cracks or fissures normally pose no great problems in themselves. However, there have been cases in which they have enlarged and continued to penetrate deeper into the pad tissue, leading to tenderness and lameness. They could also potentially act as traps for foreign matter, which could lead to further trauma and infection. As a result, if you notice a crack in a pad, manage it in the following fashion:

• For very minor, uncontaminated superficial fissures, a small amount of instant glue or adhesive applied into the crack may be used. Be certain to keep your pet from licking the area until it is completely dry.

• For deeper cracks, wash the area with soap and water. Be sure to rinse and dry well. Then seal the crack with instant glue. Note: For those cracks that appear infected or are causing obvious signs of lameness, do not apply glue. Instead, veterinary attention should be obtained.

Shampoo in the Eyes

If soap or shampoo accidentally gets into your pet's eyes during a bath, take immediate action to prevent injury to the eye.

• Flush the affected eye with copious amounts of clean water. Do not apply more ointment to the eye because this could seal in the offending agent.

• If the eye appears reddened, or if your pet is squinting or pawing at the eye, contact your veterinarian. Prevent your pet from self-traumatizing the affected eye until you reach the veterinary hospital.

Useful Addresses and Literature

Useful Literature

Davis, Karen Leigh. *Cat Handbook.* Hauppauge, NY: Barron's Educational Series, Inc., 2000.

Gleeson, Eileen and Lia Whitmore. *Ultimate Dog Grooming.* Firefly Books Ltd., 2004.

Moore, Arden. *50 Simple Ways to Pamper Your Cat.* Barnes & Noble Books, 2003.

Rice, Dan. *Dog Handbook.* Hauppauge, NY: Barron's Educational Series, Inc., 1999.

Ludwig, Gerd. *Sit! Stay!: Train Your Dog the Easy Way* (Barron's Complete Pet Owner's Manuals). Hauppauge, NY: Barron's Educational Series, Inc., 1998.

Salzberg, Kathy R. *How to Start a Home-Based Pet Care Business.* Globe Pequot Press, 2002.

Organizations and Web Sites

International Pet Groomers, Inc.
www.ipgcmg.org

American Kennel Club
www.akc.org

Cat Fanciers' Association
www.cfainc.org

National Dog Groomers Association of America
www.nationaldoggroomers.com

Pet dogs and cats depend on their owners to enhance their quality of life. Many essential grooming operations are not only easy to perform, but also enhance the human-animal bond.

Index